The End of Respectability

THE END OF RESPECTABILITY

Notes of a Black American Reckoning
with His Life and His Nation

ANTHONY WALTON

GODINE

✗ BOSTON ✗

Published in 2024 by
GODINE
Boston, Massachusetts

Several of these essays first appeared, in different form, in the following publications: *The New York Times*: "Willie Horton and Me," "Making Myths,
Betraying Our Past" (originally "American Histories: Chasing Dreams and
Nightmares; In Making Myths, Betraying Our Past"). *Seven Days*: "Riding
with the Rev." *Notre Dame Magazine*: "Letter to Jack," "After Obama" (originally "Hope at Risk"), "Reading, Writing, and the Risks of Failure." *Oxford
American*: "Prima Facie" (originally "My Secret Life as a Black Man), "Speech
at Ole Miss." *The Atlantic*: "Technology vs. African Americans." *Bowdoin
Magazine*: "Willie Horton and Me, Again."

LIBRARY OF CONGRESS CATALOGING-IN-PUBLICATION DATA
Names: Walton, Anthony, 1960- author.
Title: The end of respectability / Anthony Walton.
Description: Boston : Godine, 2024.
Identifiers: LCCN 2023050834 (print) | LCCN 2023050835 (ebook) | ISBN
  9781567927283 (hardback) | ISBN 9781567927290 (ebook)
Subjects: LCGFT: Essays.
Classification: LCC PS3573.A47268 E53 2024 (print) | LCC PS3573.A47268
  (ebook) | DDC 814/.54--dc23/eng/20240223
LC record available at https://lccn.loc.gov/2023050834
LC ebook record available at https://lccn.loc.gov/2023050835

First Printing, 2024
Printed in the United States of America

For Maren
Have I told you lately

Contents

Some of Us Are Driving a Stolen Car

An Introduction

1.

TWO OR MORE things can be simultaneously true. And in a place as large and varied as the United States, many contradictory truths can be both simultaneous and, as it were, "self-evident." Such as: America is one of the best places in the world for people of African descent, and at the same time, one of the worst.

Or, American whites are the permanent, unceasing, and near-unforgivable enemies of American Blacks and, at the same time, American Blacks can and have found nurturing, sustaining, and transformative friendships, collaborations, and romantic relationships with American whites to include forming families and raising children with them.

Parsing contradictions like these takes a lifetime, and that parsing can be very painful.

When I wrote the first essay in this book, "Willie Horton and Me," I was working from a place of acute personal distress. I had been mulling the contents of that essay for more than a year, spurred by the brutal realities I was encountering in my chosen new home, New York City. An opportunity suddenly came into being in a most unexpected fashion: I met an editor from the *New York Times Magazine*, Eric Copage, at a party at the home of a mutual friend in Harlem and brazenly asked if I might send him something. He very graciously said yes—secretly dreading the prospect, I suspect—but I went home that very evening and began writing. I poured everything I had been thinking and, more importantly, everything I had been feeling into two thousand words and mailed it off, semi-expecting that to be the end of the matter. I was shocked to hear from him a few days later that the *Times* not only wanted to publish it but wanted to do so almost immediately.

The subsequent publication of the essay on August 20, 1989, was one of the most significant events of my life. But the writing of it had been even more so. And not because I had suddenly "discovered my voice." The significance of that moment emerged because I had articulated on the page for the first time a malaise that had been slowly consuming my emotional life for years. As I relate in the essay, I was shocked—not too strong a word—by what had unfolded in the George H. W. Bush campaign in 1988: specifically, the use of the convict Willie Horton in a commercial that was, in my opinion, specifically designed to portray Democratic candidate Michael Dukakis as "soft on crime" by flagrantly fanning a fear of Black men and diminishing their status as an integral part of America's pluralistic society. I had thought of Bush as a good guy (at least as far as post-Nixon Republicans went), and I had respected his father, Prescott, as a Republican who had done at least *something* to help us. So it was all the more shocking to see him stoop so low, using the tactics of a predatory demagogue. I had spent much of the '80s, the Reagan years, coming to terms with the realization that most of what I had been taught—or fed—about American life and society was wrong.

I was born in a time and place to parents who came from marginalized social circumstances. Their hard-won position in the Chicago middle-class gave me a vision of America that was not wrong, or even necessarily untrue, but that was at best incomplete. And incomplete in ways that were damaging and very dangerous—at times literally—to me. It wasn't really anybody's fault. My parents had had to operate with limited knowledge, resources, and social capital. Given how little they started with in Depression Mississippi, what they eventually accomplished was astounding and worthy of only honor and praise. But they had been operating within crippling limitations, restrictions that prevented me from seeing my country as clearly as I would need to given my dreams and goals.

Geographically, I was from a section of the country that, I now realize, shielded me from some of the realities of American life, especially for American Blacks. Growing up in Northern Illinois, raised by churchgoing strivers who believed in working hard and fitting in, who preached to me and my siblings that a secure place in America could be earned, I was less aware of how difficult things were for many Blacks, particularly in urban ghettos and the Deep South. I knew, anecdotally, that there were many problems that remained to be solved, but in my own family story and experience, we had progressed, and we were getting there.

We had learned how to manage the racist micro- and macro-aggressions we had encountered in our section of Illinois, Kane and DuPage Counties, and we had also learned that there were white people who would work with us as friends and equals.

I think of the bankers, real estate agents, teachers, and guidance counselors who provided us with credit, service, and information as we made our way forward, first my parents from the late 1950s, then me and my brother and sister into the '60s, '70s, and '80s. In some ways I am grateful for what might be thought of as the naivete this engendered because it allowed me to develop both ambition and confidence; I didn't feel the circumscription I might have felt if I had grown up in the Chicago Housing Authority of the 1960s and '70s or the Roxbury that was under siege from the busing "crisis" in Boston. And I didn't face the crack epidemic in Brooklyn and Queens or the gang wars of South Central. I was allowed a little running space, just enough to see myself as an individual and to make my way forward.

As a young man, I attended the University of Notre Dame and then earned a graduate degree from Brown University and was, I thought, ready for the world. I progressed in various ways, but I also began to notice various genres of racism—some subtle, some overt, some so brutal I had to worry if I was "imagining" what I saw, and all of it much more intense than what I had experienced before. Knocking heads with police. Landlords shutting me out with a light touch and not-so-light touch. Being followed by security guards in hotels, apartment buildings, and banks and not being allowed in retail stores in New York City. The parent of a white acquaintance telling me, clearly, not to come back to their house after I had been invited. And the classic circumstance that became such a trope of African American experience that it is now a cliché: my inability, no matter how corporately attired and equipped, to get a taxi, especially in Manhattan. I have come to understand this everyday hazing as an initial encounter with worlds in which I was not "special": I was not the cherished son of local stalwarts, I was not a privileged and prized student at an elite university. I was, for the first time, just another Black man on the street.

The concussive effect of these low-grade traumas had reached a crescendo of psychic tension by the evening I met Mr. Copage in New York. I had something to say, and in what was in some ways a form of personal therapy and release, I said it. But at the time I also continued to have a modicum of hope that it might be "solved." I was, in 1989, close enough to the concrete gains of "I Have a Dream" and the Civil Rights Movement that I thought American racial dysfunction could and would be turned around. If only people knew what was happening, they would realize that there were things that could be done, and they would do them. I wrote "Willie Horton and Me" with what I thought was a warning—perhaps a prophecy—but I still believed there was a chance for, if not that postracial paradise where conflict and division no longer existed, at least an atmosphere of comity, tolerance, and cooperation that we as Americans could build on, and that we as African Americans could live with: something *close enough* to Dr. Martin Luther King Jr.'s Dream. A situation in which, if we were not fully appreciated participants in the fabled melting pot, we would at least progress beyond being the fabled "pot" itself, the caste against which all other groups measured their status in American society. Then, twenty years later, the election of Barack Obama made me think that perhaps such a resolution was nigh.

I remember watching Obama and his family on the stage in Grant Park in Chicago on November 4, 2008, the night he won the presidency. That a Black man had been comfortably elected president felt like a pivot in history, a moment after which nothing would be the same. And I was right, just not in the fashion that I was thinking. Because *then* came the Tea Party, the manifestation and physical embodiment of steadily accelerating white supremacy, paranoia, and backlash; the unrelenting attacks of the Republican Party and Fox News along with the rest of the right-wing media ecosystem; and after that, the chaotic apotheosis of Trumpism.

In the most tragic of ironies, the transformative election of Obama had unleashed a ferocity of white resentment and hate that I had not foreseen or imagined possible. That resentment has come to define the last fifteen years of our society, and it has the possibility of defining, warping, and even endangering the next fifty to one hundred years of our country's future. At the risk of seeming alarmist, I think it might even be the bleeding edge of an ultimate collapse.

I have sometimes thought that Obama arose twenty-five years too soon, that if Americans could have had one more generation of quiet progress and normalization, if we could have gone twenty-five more years without calling up the devils and demons of racial strife and other kinds of hatred in the installation of an African American president in the White House, with its soft iconographic echo of the plantation's "Big House," the nation might have turned the corner. But that was not to be our fate, and it might not even be true. I find myself believing that the sort of white grievances we see embodied in Trumpism are something that is encoded in the double helix of the American body politic, something that sometimes sleeps but is always there, the malignant dragon that cannot be slain. So Obama was elected, the current backlash began, and we saw the rise of Trump—making the Willie Horton ads and Republican race-baiting in the '70s and '80s begin to seem like rather small fry in light of what was to come.

But we now see the truth. Those of us who do not want polarization and unending conflict—those Blacks, whites, Latinx, Asians, and LGBTQ who dream of, if not the Peaceable Kingdom, then simply getting home after work and grilling salmon or burgers quietly on the patio and not caring who lives in the neighborhood as long as they cut the grass—now know what's out there, good and bad. And with this information we can build and hope that maybe the next lurch forward in racial progress will not be made by men and women as naive as I was as a young man.

2.

SINCE 1989 I HAVE been writing and reporting period-ically about race, often at the behest of an editor. I have been asked to go somewhere and look into something that has happened, to contemplate and offer my thoughts on a mat-ter of the moment, or to more generally offer observations on racial history, context, and current conditions. I have served as a domestic correspondent on what might be called the "state" of race within America. While I have written about a great many other things over the decades, I have always found myself drifting back to thinking about the ways, means, and mores of race as the ethical contradiction inscribed in the country's founding with which we are still reckoning. It is the revenant of our past most felt in our present, the inheritance we cannot dispossess or fully remedy.

We fight the wars we inherit. As a proud descendant of both Mississippi and Chicagoland, I most definitely was born into a war. I refer to the American Civil War, which in my view has never ended. It has only morphed into a series of less announced, more fragmented, and more irregular but still lethal conflicts. Reconstruction, Jim Crow, the Civil Rights Movement, the Reagan Revolution, the Tea Party, and now MAGA Trumpism have all been, at their core, struggles about whether or not American Blacks would remain "less than." And every step of progress for African Americans has been met with vicious reply, sometimes violently with lynchings and in "white rebellions" such as the Tulsa Race Massacre of 1921, and sometimes through systemic, systematic legal regimes, rules, practices, covenants, and cultural practices that sought to keep us from owning, accumulating, and bequeathing what we once were: property.

If I hadn't been born African American and concomitantly grown up in middle-class circumstances with privilege that allowed me to observe and ponder different aspects and geographies of the United States, I probably wouldn't have chosen to spend my life thinking so obsessively about these matters. One of my life goals has been that my daughter not have to think so preemptively and obsessively about race, which I do not think I will be able to guarantee. But I have lived my life, and my thoughts, as I came to them—I was born to a certain couple in a certain town in a certain state who were from a certain place and time and who were living out those collective contingencies. And I inherited their fights and vulnerabilities as well as their hopes and dreams and, I now realize, their terrors and fears.

I published "Willie Horton and Me" one week before my twenty-ninth birthday. Three days later, Yusuf Hawkins was murdered on a street corner in Brooklyn. It was a particularly horrific racial crime—lynching is not too strong a word—in the most cosmopolitan city in the United States *in* 1989. Yet I fear that the killing, and the innocent young man, have been forgotten. Looking back, I see that August of 1989 was a moment of baptism for me. I had always dreamed of becoming a writer, but I hadn't expected my initiation to occur in quite the way it had transpired nor alongside Hawkins's murder in the city in which I lived and worked. My essay generated more than five hundred letters to the editor (and to me) and several death threats. It came to take on a life of its own.

Around that time, I was asked by Adam Moss and Patricia Towers at *Seven Days* to write a brief story about the Reverend Al Sharpton, who was rapidly solidifying a position as a civil rights persona unlike any that had ever been seen before. Unlike the credentialed and respectability-obsessed earlier generations of twentieth century civil rights leaders such as W. E. B. Du Bois, Dr. Martin Luther King Jr., and Whitney Young, Sharpton was a further extension of his friend and mentor Jesse Jackson but was even more cynical and "street." He also had an evident love of the Black masses, and average Black people trusted him. He seized leadership of the protests surrounding the Hawkins killing, and I spent several days with him, traveling throughout the city and observing an entirely different way of being Black and standing up to both the white and Black establishments.

Over the next thirty years, Sharpton would become an ever more famous if limited-in-effectiveness Black leader, mastering the media and its various processes and using that mastery to manipulate it in ways that I think even Dr. King would have admired. Sharpton was in some ways a somewhat diminished simulacrum of Dr. King, but he was also intermittently successful and sometimes profound, and I think if he had been able to publicly apologize for his unseemly role in the tragic-all-around Tawana Brawley affair, he might have become the undisputed Black power broker of his time. (In 1987, Ms. Brawley, a Black teenager, falsely accused four white men of rape. Sharpton vehemently—and, it was later revealed, wrongly—sided with Ms. Brawley.) Sharpton's actions and what might be described as arrogance during the situation alienated most whites and many mainstream Blacks. (I worked with Sharpton as co-author for an autobiography he published in the early '90s.)

Sharpton, whatever his flaws, remains a trusted and even beloved figure in the Black neighborhoods and ghettos of the United States. There he was, the day of the George Floyd verdict in 2021, standing at the courthouse with George Floyd's brother and Benjamin Crump. And then a few days later he was delivering the eulogy for and comforting the mother of Daunte Wright, another young Black man in Minnesota who died in an altercation with the police.

I think my subsequent journey as a person and an American, as well as a writer of nonfiction and an observer of racial politics, can be traced by the essays in this book, as roughly my journey from "Willie Horton and Me" to "The End of Respectability." You might also interpret these writings as roughly parallel to the passage of much of the nation from, say, the Rodney King beating and Los Angeles Riots in 1992 to the George Floyd murder and the nationwide protests, with Barack Obama's presidency and much else (to include the ascent of Michael Jordan and Tiger Woods, the Nicole Brown Simpson and Ronald Goldman murders, and the colonization of pop culture by hip-hop) along the way.

And though much has been endured and suffered in the sixty years of my lifetime, much has also been gained, and therein we will find the theme of this book. I started my journey in bewildered pain and rage and have finished with what I hope are confident, measured conclusions. My arrival at qualified certainties about racial matters means that I am no longer willing to "beseech" and ask for understanding from those white readers who would deny African Americans their basic humanity. As an African American, I went from "WTF?" in 1989 to "We ain't having it" in 2024, which is also a path that I think many African Americans have traveled. And in truth, I think many whites have traveled that road as well, as evidenced by the crowds protesting in memory of George Floyd in 2020 and the steady core of decency that can be seen day by day all around our nation, even in the face of police violence, economic dislocation, health care disparities, and MAGA and QAnon's growing paranoia and rage.

3.

OVER THE THIRTY-FIVE YEARS I have been writing about race, I began to utilize an acutely apt cliché for our racial circumstances: the more things change, the more they stay the same. That statement is painfully true but also not complex enough to encompass the whole truth of our country's struggle with racism because in America there is, undeniably, most certainly change. Life has improved a great deal for African Americans since World War II, since 1954, since 1965, since 1996. Life has also declined, as can be ascertained by the most cursory glance at the urban and rural deprivation endured by large numbers of Blacks who have been basically set aside and forgotten in our national psychomachia.

Two steps forward, three steps back. Blacks served as equals in World War II, were *allowed* to fight alongside whites for the first time, and they showcased great skill and valor. Yet those same veterans were greeted by both blistering and subtle resistance upon their return when they tried to partake as full members of American society. In horrific events as gruesome as the blinding of Isaac Woodard and the murder of Medgar Evers, and in the quietly ruthless postwar racial housing covenants and mortgage redlining supported by the federal government, there were forces determined that Blacks not advance. Only these weren't *forces—*

there is nothing supernatural about them. They were and are *policies*: the collective attitudes and activities of humans, imposed punitively upon other humans.

Each time the nation attempts to deal with this pattern, we enact a series of pantomimes and feints that provide just enough wiggle room for a certain percentage of Blacks to take a few steps forward in society, but which also allow many—most?—whites to evade any serious accounting of what has happened, what is happening, and what needs to be considered and done to move toward an equitable future. But I acknowledge that some of the white failure to fully reckon with the past (and present) has been inadvertent for a number of reasons, such as the substantial group of whites who live in locales that are not subsumed or poisoned by racial matters (out of sight, out of mind). And some of it is unintentional, just the residue and bad luck of our snake-bit national history. But some of it is quite deliberate and has always been so, from the cataclysmic 1877 sellout of the first Reconstruction by then-presidential candidate Rutherford B. Hayes up through the deliberate exclusion of Blacks from various New Deal benefits through Nixon's and Bush's Southern Strategy to contemporary attacks on so called "wokeism," the 1619 Project, CRT, and DEI. The dragon of racial hatred appears in each generation with a new mien and menace but virtually the same existential threat to Black lives.

We stay locked in a loop, a Möbius strip of our own making, and are therefore always in a state of reconstruction—and I fear that this pattern will never end. I think of our nation as currently undergoing a Third Reconstruction, the Second being the King years, with our present activity precipitated by the murder of George Floyd. I fully expect there to be fourth, fifth, sixth and seventh reconstructions into the infinite American future—for as long as there is an America, an assumption we can no longer safely make.

4.

I DO HAVE A theory as to why we are trapped in this repetition compulsion or *Groundhog Day* of racial trauma, and why it is so difficult to achieve legitimately transformative advancement. It's actually kind of simple.

I think some middle- and working-class whites are caught in a sort of double bind: they have become accustomed to thinking of themselves as "white," which in the United States (and through much of Western civilization) has come to signify accomplishment, power, and most of all, superiority. And for a certain segment of whites in America and the western hemisphere, that is certainly true. For less accomplished, impoverished, or disenfranchised whites, it must be a terrible psychic burden to carry mental expectations of, shall we say, supremacy while not in any fashion being able to experience its material or experiential dividends. For me, this is a significant portion of the energy driving the phenomenon now known as Trumpism. If you believe that your natural patrimony is to be economically on top and you are not, someone must have robbed you of your birthright. Who could that be?

Part of the diabolical magic of Donald Trump is his ability to assure a crucial portion of the white community that they have in fact been robbed of their patrimony—

their just deserts, economic and cultural—by Blacks, by Mexicans, by Muslims, by gay and transgender people. It has been his genius to articulate, with brutal simplicity, what has been assumed for decades, if not centuries, if not since the beginning of European settlement and Manifest Destiny: *We are destined to achieve our city on a hill and to be recognized for our moral election and material power.* But someone has interrupted that reign for whites who do not find themselves living atop that hill, and Trump, like Hitler, offers them scapegoats with force and entertainment. He's allegedly a tough guy but also a hoot—a bankrupted charlatan turned reality TV star.

Finally, I also think a certain number of whites are acting from fear. To put it simply, they see the demographic numbers changing and worry about being outnumbered and overpowered—at the ballot box, in their neighborhoods and workplaces, in society at large. Also, I think in their darkest imaginations they are aware of how people of color, Blacks especially, have been treated throughout history and up to this very moment, and they worry that they will be treated in the same detrimental ways that they have treated (and often still want to treat) Blacks.

They see themselves in an existential conflict and view those of us who still value Dr. King's vision as mortal threats either consciously (as in white nationalists and white supremacists) or unconsciously (as in certain evangelicals, MAGA revelers, and QAnon conspiracy adherents). But it all comes down to *which* Americans have their patrimony and hard work stolen from them. And this leads me to a different formulation: What if our racial conflicts and misunderstandings are rooted in theft? What if contemporary whites who feel cheated of economic superiority are in fact "innocent" in a certain way?

I do think millions of white Americans are not necessarily guilty of the crimes of the past. If you are a contemporary white Oklahoman, or to be even more specific, a white Tulsan, of course you did not perpetrate the 1921 Tulsa Race Massacre—but you are living with the ill-gotten gains of it. You are, as they would say on *Law & Order*, an accessory after the fact.

Think of it this way: your grandfather had in his possession a very special car, a bitching cherry-red 1965 Corvette (or a Shelby Mustang, or a 2002 BMW, or a 1950s Ford pickup—take your pick), and he loved it and transferred his love of the vehicle to you. You and he rode around town in that car, ate ice cream in it, and maybe he even taught you to drive in it. Those wheels were part of your life, even part of the family. He had it for most of his life, and he promised it to you. And he kept his promise: in his will he left his beloved car to you. This is, so far, a very lovely story.

Then, years later, you find out that your grandfather, whom you worshipped and thought was the best man you had ever known, had, in fact, stolen that Corvette. He never owned it because he and his friends robbed a Black man, or a Native American, or a Latino, or an Asian, to steal it. This happened in the past, during an era in which law enforcement was known to look the other way. In your case, maybe law enforcement, in the shape of one of your grandfather's closest friends, helped him steal it. Perhaps they—or he—even killed the rightful owner.

Suddenly, you learn that you have been driving a stolen car, one that has a history not only of theft but of murder.

Now, what do you do?

Do you give it back?

Do you say, *Well, that's unfortunate, but that was a very long time ago?*

Do you let the descendants of the unfortunate rightful owner of color drive it once a month?

Do you stand on a street corner downtown and proclaim your innocence because you didn't know the provenance of your cherished car? Do you claim that even if the story of its illicit theft is true, it doesn't change anything?

Do you go to court and sue, arguing that giving it back unfairly infringes upon your property and opportunity rights?

Do you argue that laws must be passed demanding that unlawful generational theft not be discussed and that anyone who brings such things up is looking backward and trying to make your kids feel poorly about themselves, and as such they should be silenced?

Do you insist that only your version of events, which implies that the larceny and homicide never happened, can be discussed? Do you argue that if this theft did, in fact, happen, you don't know anything about it and therefore have absolutely no legal, moral, or ethical responsibility? 'Cause, man, that is one beautiful car, and it's great to be the one that gets to drive it, and you know you're very lucky, but like your grandfather said, the Lord rewards those who deserve to be rewarded. The fact that you have it means you are supposed to have it, and the people who don't have it are just undeserving sore losers.

This is the ethos of Calvinist election and the prosperity gospel, and like most feel-good mythmaking ideology, it is self-justification—an enabling fiction that flies in the face of fact.

5.

THE PRECEDING ANALOGY IS, in a nutshell, why I don't think our racial conflict and trauma can be *resolved*. We're in a cosmic trap, not exactly of our own devising, but one that we as a nation do not have the moral vision or fortitude to grapple with in any sort of meaningful way. We ameliorate around the edges, we try to help Black people and other people of color as we can—so long as it doesn't affect our own comfort and security—and the most ambitious of us wonder if the way to lessen white grievance is to include white people in that amelioration. Assuming that there were the political consensus to implement the much-bandied "class not race" reformation of our society, how many of the *white* beneficiaries of such an arrangement would accept it? Enough to depolarize and reestablish equilibrium in our society? Wouldn't that force the aggressively populist Trumpist portion of them to concede some of the psychic benefits of their red-hatted whiteness? Wouldn't they have to admit they were on the same socioeconomic plane as many Blacks and other people of color and therefore forfeit the escapist benefits of membership in a fictional America that had been made, once again, "great"?

I remember reading the essays of James Baldwin as a young man. I was fired up by their prophetic powers and inspired by the possibilities of American healing that they often yearned for. He gave me hope in a kind of tidal progress that I have often contemplated as a Chicagoan who has, for the last thirty years, made coastal Maine my home. Meditating on the craggy Maine shoreline, its geology worn by eras of sea change, I would think of this passage in Baldwin's writing, which had spoken to me as a young person, not yet disabused of his ideals:

> For nothing is fixed, forever and forever, it is not fixed; the earth is always shifting, the light is always changing, the sea does not cease to grind down rock. Generations do not cease to be born, and we are responsible to them because we are the only witnesses they have. The sea rises, the light falls, lovers cling to each other and children cling to us. The moment we cease to hold each other, the moment we break faith with one another, the sea engulfs us and the light goes out.

There is, I believe, an immense amount of witnessed truth in that statement, but I also can't say, as someone in late middle age, that I have maintained such fervor and hope. I do recognize the progress that African Americans have made and, importantly, the progress that has been made *on our behalf* by the wider society. I am willing to say that if African Americans have progressed, then our society has progressed. But what will it take for that progress to *feel* like bedrock gains? And what will it take for right-wing whites to not think that any Black progress is, by definition, a cause of their suffering?

So much has changed, for the better, in ways that my grandparents could not and would not have dared imagine. But is it enough? Is it truly transformational? And if it is, why are the material measurables for Blacks compared to other groups so bad? Why is there always backlash to any mention of Black advance, and why are there always riven racial conflicts, overt and covert, large and small? Why are Blacks always painted as "stealing," undeserving, a threat? Why am I, by certain segments of the population, still perceived as Willie Horton rather than your average father: commuting to work, spending time with his beloved daughter, voting and paying his taxes, getting the car tuned up and inspected at prescribed intervals, and listening to both Bach and Bob Marley? Why does my Blackness matter more than anything else?

6.

As I was writing this book in the summer of 2023, yet another racial tempest emerged, this one involving Kathleen McElroy, an esteemed journalist, editor, and professor who had recently been recruited to Texas A&M, her alma mater, to direct the journalism program and build it to a stature that would reflect the importance of the university in the state and, increasingly, the nation. Dr. McElroy is a former editor at the *New York Times* and had previously been an esteemed professor at the University of Texas at Austin (UT). All seemed to be in order for her move to A&M, and she had been led to believe that the university was excited to have her join the faculty. Then, outside conservative groups began interfering with the hire, complaining that McElroy's previous comments about the need for more Black professors in American academia rendered her unfit

for a job at A&M. The resulting scandal led to the resigna-
tion of both the president and dean of the university after
McElroy decided to decline the appointment and return to
UT, and the faculty senate demanded an investigation into
how and why an otherwise acclaimed addition to the faculty had been scuttled.

This story, in a nutshell, reflects the concerns and
themes of this book. Dr. McElroy, an African American
and the daughter of a celebrated military family, had spent
her career participating without complaint—and with
admirable distinction—in mainstream society, garnering
a master's from NYU and a PhD from the University of
Texas, in addition to her BA from A&M. She worked as a
journalist for thirty years, finishing at the *Times*, where she
held several management and editorial positions. She then
became a professor at Oklahoma State before joining UT.

The treatment she suffered reveals several truths.
First, could there be a resume that more clearly reflected
the "work hard and play by the rules and you will succeed
in America" ethos of the contemporary GOP? And can
one truly run afoul of the "woke" police merely by expressing such a benign opinion as the idea that there should
be more Black professors? When I wrote "Willie Horton
and Me," one of the things that most troubled me was the
dawning suspicion that no matter what I did, no matter
how hard I worked, no matter what credentials I accrued,
it would not be enough: I would never be fully accepted as
an American. And here, in 2023, is the replication of a similar circumstance that legitimates my persistent fear. When
right-wingers and MAGA nuts complain that Blacks
are suspicious of their motives and refuse to give them a

chance, I recommend that the treatment of Dr. McElroy be a case study in why that is so.

I have been alive for what feels like a long time; I was seven years old the night when Dr. Martin Luther King Jr. was assassinated. I have lived through Reagan and Obama, through Warren Buffett and Steve Jobs, through Oprah and Michael Jordan. I felt the exhilaration of Obama and the cognitive dislocation of MAGA and QAnon. But it seems to me that the two most important Americans in my lifetime are Donald Trump and George Floyd, men who have come to represent things beyond a single human life and who could not have had more different lives. Yet they crystallize, in tragically different ways, the two most crucial and opposed aspects of America.

Trump, with his pathologically narcissistic disregard for anything that does not directly serve or benefit him, symbolizes the America that is incapable of understanding itself and making the adjustments that might help us manage the chaotic spiraling crises of climate change, racial strife, inadequate health care systems, and immigration. Floyd, on the other hand, represents those left behind and disregarded, the other half so forgotten that a police officer could execute him in the middle of the street as cameras roll with no concern for the consequences. None of it makes any sense.

Race, race, race. Some Americans of every stripe have tired of these discussions and have tired of writers like me who keep asking questions and making demands. But it seems a simple thing to reason that if race were a crucial portion of the *making* of America (slavery, three-fifths of a person, the Civil War, Jim Crow), it would then (also) be a crucial part of the *unmaking* of America.

Race remains a threat to our stability because it is a flaw in the laws of our foundational physics. I think of various American belief systems derived from Greek mythology, Judeo-Christianity, Islam, physics, Rawlsian justice, and evolutionary biology. They all imply that, in one way or another, events will find their balance. In terms of human morality and racial justice, things have been radically out of balance in America for more than four hundred years. In my view, it doesn't take a great deal of contemplation to reason that perhaps the scales are starting to strain toward a new balance.

Time is wasting. If we cannot solve this soon, we are risking literally everything—it is not too much to assert that current conditions threaten the planet and the continuance of human life. Climate change requires cooperation on every level, in every phase of American society, and across the globe. The petty GOP strategies and policies that are based upon racial fear and prejudice—while accruing to the benefit of plutocratic energy, media, and financial billionaires—not only threaten the racial, spiritual, and moral health of the nation but also the material health and natural systems of the planet. It is time, as a nation, to grow up, to put away childish things, as Saint Paul demanded. Black folks are not going anywhere, nor are any other groups of color, nor are women, nor are LGBTQ folks, nor are women with aspirations beyond the home. The politics of division, fear, and spite are only delaying the inevitable; they will make the various crashes and collapses that are looming as climate change and its concomitant disasters coalesce (such as migrant and refugee tragedies, storm survival, and infrastructure rehabilitation) that much more violent and costly.

I think about the protests in the wake of the murder of George Floyd and how many of the Americans crowding the streets were young whites, refusing to accept such egregious brutal behavior, standing against evil and speaking truth to power. I think of my own family, which leapt in one generation from sharecroppers to professionals, finding work as college professors, suburban educational administrators, and members of law enforcement. As I wrote earlier, I don't think we will ever get there in terms of racial reconciliation, but I do think there can be marginal improvement in all measurable—and, by extension, immeasurable—factors, day by day, month by month, year by year, decade by decade. What that will require is for the white, Black, Latino, Asian, Native American, and LGBTQ people of the United States who want to live peaceably with each other to reconceive of their bonds and assert themselves in a political coalition that can speak effectively to those goals.

And I think that can be good enough. It will have to be.

The End of Respectability

Willie Horton and Me

I AM A BLACK man. I am a Black man, born, let's say,
between *Brown v. Board of Education* in 1954 and the
Mississippi burning murders of Schwerner, Chaney,
and Goodman in 1964. Or, in the years that followed the
murder of Emmett Till in 1955, but before the murder of Dr.
Martin Luther King Jr. in 1968.

I am one of the young Black Americans Dr. King sang
of in his "I Have A Dream" speech: "I have a dream that . . .
the sons of former slaves and the sons of former slave owners will be able to sit down together at the table of broth-
erhood . . . that my four little children will one day live
in a nation where they will not be judged by the color of
their skin, but by the content of their character . . . I have
a dream today!"

Though I have a living memory of Dr. King, I don't remember hearing that speech live. I do remember my parents,

relatives, teachers, and professors endlessly recounting it, exhorting me to live up to the dream, to pick up the ball of freedom, as it were, and run with it, because one day, I was assured, we would look up and the dream would be a reality.

I like to think I lived up to my part of the bargain. I stayed in school and remained home many nights when I didn't have to in the interest of staying out of trouble. I endured a lonely Catholic school education because public school wasn't good enough for my parents' (or my) aspirations for me. At Notre Dame and Brown, I endured further isolation, and I burned the midnight oil, as Dr. King had urged.

I am sure that I represent one of the best efforts that Americans, Black Americans particularly, have made to live up to Dr. King's dream. I have a white education, a white accent, I conform to white middle-class standards in virtually every choice, from preferring Brooks Brothers oxford cloth to religiously clutching my gold cards as the tickets to the good life. I'm not complaining about any of that. The world, even the white world, has been, if not good, then acceptable to me. But as I get older, I feel that I failed to notice something, or that I've been deceived. I couldn't put my finger on it until I met Willie Horton.

George H. W. Bush and his henchmen could not have invented Willie Horton. Horton, with his coal-Black skin, huge, unkempt Afro, and a glare that would have given Bull Connor or Lester Maddox serious pause, had committed a brutal murder in 1974 and been sentenced to life in prison. Then, granted a weekend furlough from prison in 1987, Horton viciously raped a white woman in front of her fiancé, who was also attacked.

Willie Horton was the perfect symbol of what happened to innocent whites when Democrats were on the watch, at least in the gospel according to post-Goldwater Republicans. Horton himself, in just a fuzzy mug shot, gave even the stoutest, most open, liberal heart a shiver. Even mine. I thought of all the late nights I had ridden in terror on the F and A trains while living in New York City. I thought Willie Horton must be what the wolf packs I had often heard about, but never seen, must look like. I said to myself, "Something has got to be done about these criminals."

Then, one night, a temporary doorman at my Greenwich Village high-rise refused to let me pass. And it occurred to me that it had taken the regular doormen—Black, white, Hispanic—months to adjust to my coming and going. Then a friend's landlord in Brooklyn asked if I was living in his apartment. We had been working on a screenplay under deadline, and I was there several days in a row. The landlord said she didn't mind, but the neighbors . . . Then one day I was late for the Metroliner, heading for Harvard and a weekend with several yuppie, buppie, and guppie friends. I stood, in blazer and khakis, in front of the New York University Law School for thirty minutes, unable to get a cab. As it started to rain, I realized I was not going to get a cab.

Soaking wet, I gave up on the Metroliner and trudged home. As I cleaned up, I looked in the mirror. Wet, my military haircut looked slightly unkempt. My eyes were red from the water and stress. I couldn't help thinking, *If Willie got a haircut and cooled out* . . . If Willie Horton would become just a little middle class, he would look like me.

☙❧

FOR YOUNG BLACKS OF my sociological cohort, it could seem as though racism was often an abstract thing, ancient history, at worst a stone against which to whet our combat skills as we went winging through the world proving our superiority. We were the children of The Dream. Incidents in my childhood and adolescence were steadfastly, often laughingly, overcome by a combination of the fresh euphoria of the Civil Rights Movements and the exhortations and Christian piety of my mother. Now, in retrospect, I can see that racism has always been with me, even when I was shielded by love or money, or when I chose not to see it. But I saw it in the face of Willie Horton, and I can't ignore it, because it is my face.

Willie Horton has taught me the continuing need for a skill W. E. B. Du Bois outlined and perfected one hundred years ago: living with the veil. I am recognizing my veil of double-consciousness, my American-self and my Black-self. I must battle, like all humans, to see myself. I must also battle, because I am Black, to see myself as others see me; increasingly, my life, literally, depends upon it. I might meet notorious gunman Bernhard Goetz or someone like him on the subway; my car might break down in a neighborhood like Howard Beach, where a young Black man had been killed several years earlier; the armed security guard might mistake me for a burglar in the lobby of my building. And they won't see a mild-mannered English major trying to get home. They will see Willie Horton. My father was born in a tar paper, tin roof shack on a cotton plantation near Holly Springs, Mississippi. His father was a sharecropper. *His* father had been born a slave. My father came north, and by dint of a ferocity I still find frightening, carved an economic space for himself that became a launchpad to the Ivy League, to art school, to professional school, for his children.

As the song by John Cougar Mellencamp says it, "Ain't that America . . ." But a closer look reveals that each of my father's children is in some way dangerously disgruntled, perhaps irrevocably alienated from the country, *their* country, that twenty-five years ago held so much promise. And the friends of my father's children, the children of the dream Dr. King died to preserve, a collection of people ranging from investment bankers to sidemen for Miles Davis, are, to a man and woman, actively unsatisfied.

Du Bois, in *The Souls of Black Folk*, posed a question perhaps more painful today than in 1903: "Training for life teaches living; but what training for the profitable living together of Black and white?"

I think we, the children of The Dream, often feel as if we are holding thirty-year bonds that have matured and are suddenly worthless. There is a feeling, spoken and unspoken, of having been suckered. This distaste is festering into bitterness. I know that I disregarded jeering and opposition from young Blacks in adolescence as I led a "square," even dreary, life predicated on a coming harvest from keeping-one's-nose-clean. And now I see that I am often treated the same as a thug, that no amount of conformity, willing or unwilling, will make me the fabled American individual. I think it has something to do with Willie Horton.

BLACK YOUTH CULTURE IN 1989 was increasingly an expression of alienation and disgust with any mainstream (or so-called white) values. Or notions. Cameo haircuts, rap music, outsize jewelry were merely symptoms of attitudes that at the time I thought were probably beyond changing, and I think if anything that alienation has become more extreme. My Black Ivy League friends and myself were, and in many cases still are, manifesting attitudes infinitely more contemptuous and insidious; I don't know of one who is doing much more on the subject of Dr. King's dream than cynically biding his or her time, waiting for some as-yet-unidentified apocalypse that will enable us to slay the white dragon, even as we work for it, live next to it, and sleep with it. And I fear we have watched our children develop similar—if, of course, generationally different in their realizations—versions of those cynicisms.

Our dissatisfaction is leading us to despise the white dragon rather than the dragon of racism, but how can we do otherwise when everywhere we look, we see Willie Horton?

And we must acknowledge progress. Even in our darkest, most paranoid moments, we can acknowledge white friends and lovers. I wouldn't have survived the series of white institutions that has been my conscious life without them. But it is hard to acknowledge *any* progress, because whites like to use the smallest increment of change to deny what we see as the totality. And, even in the most perfect and loving interracial relationships, racism waits like a cancer, ready to wake and consume the relationship at any, even the most innocuous, time. My best friend, white and Jewish, will never understand why I was ready to start World War III over perceived slights at an American Express office. In my darker moments, I suspect he is a bit afraid of me now. In my darkest moments, I wonder if even he sees Willie Horton.

Some of you are by now, sincerely or cynically, asking yourselves, "But what does he want?" A friend of mine says that the complaints of today's young Blacks are indeed different from those of generations ago because it is very difficult to determine whether this alienation is a clarion call for the next phase of the Civil Rights Movement or merely the whining of spoiled and corrupted minority elites who could be placated by a larger share in the fruits of a corrupt and exploitative system that would continue to enslave the majority of their brothers and sisters.

I don't think there is any answer to that question. I also think that the very fact that it can be asked points to the unique character of the American race question, and the unhealable breach that manifests itself as a result in our culture and society. I don't think, for good or bad, that in any other ethnic group the fate of an individual is so inextricably bound to that of the group, and vice versa. To use the symbol and metaphor of Willie Horton in another way, I do not think that the lives and choices of white males are impacted by the existence of neo-Nazi skinheads, murdering Klansmen, or the ordinary thugs of Howard Beach. I also, to put it plainly, do not recall any young Black man, even those who deal drugs in such places, entering a playground and spraying bullets at innocent schoolchildren, as happened in Stockton, California, in 1989, months after the ads and months before I wrote this essay, or entering a church and slaughtering innocents as they prayed, as happened at Mother Emanuel church in Charleston in 2015. It is not my intention to place value considerations on *any* of these events. I want to point out that in this society it seems legitimate, from the loftiest corridors of power to the streets of New York, to imply that one Black man is them all.

And I want to be extraordinarily careful not to demonize Willie Horton. He should not be a symbol or scapegoat for our sins; he is a tragically troubled man—troubled like thousands of others, Black and white—who was unwittingly used by a presidential candidate to further division and misunderstanding. If anything, Horton is a particularly precise example of the willingness of those in power to pit us against one another. One lately fashionable statement, about to slide from truth to truism, is that Blacks have the most to fear from lawless Blacks. Any clear-eyed perusal of crime statistics will prove this. But what does it avail if the media—if a presidential candidate—use this ongoing tragedy merely to antagonize and further separate Americans?

I think that what I am finally angry about is my realization of a certain hollowness at the center of American life.

Earlier, I mentioned the sense of having undergone a hoax. That hoax, as I now see it, is that the American community is putatively built upon the fundamentals of liberty and justice for all, that it is to be expected that the freedom to compete will result in winners and losers, and that the goal of society is to ensure the fairness of opportunity. In light of the events of recent years, I begin to see that we are, competing or not, winners or not, irrevocably chained together, Black and white, rich and poor. New York City is a glaring microcosm of this interrelatedness, which can be thought of as either a web of fear ensnaring and enslaving us, or as a net of mutuality that strengthens us all.

As events like the Central Park jogger rape case illustrate, the world is becoming ever smaller, and it is increasingly difficult to consign social problems to realms outside our personal arenas of concern. In that tragic incident, what might otherwise have been a local, albeit horrific, crime, can become, because of the mythic aspects of the details—in this case, an innocent young white woman being brutally gang-raped, allegedly by young black men—a global story publicized by third and fourth parties for sinister reasons of their own that have nothing to do with the original crime. And that may hinder law enforcement in solving the crime. And it may fan rage and anger, in that case falsely, against Black men who must live with societal fallout *from something that is not true.* This happens again and again. I see the connection between Willie Horton and me because it affects my own liberty. It was not always an obvious connection.

Another quote from Dr. King brings the issue into focus: "Most of the gains . . . were obtained at bargain rates. The desegregation of public facilities cost nothing; neither did the election and appointment of a few Black public officials." To move to the next level of progress, we must face the fact that there are going to be costs, especially economic costs. To hire two Black firefighters means two white firefighters won't be hired, and this is no easy reality. Racism is ultimately based on power and greed, the twin demons of most human frailties. These demons cannot be scapegoated, as the saga of Willie Horton proves. They are more like the many-headed Hydra, and will haunt our dreams, waking and other, regardless.

Riding with the Rev

"We come today to bury one of our children. It would be easy to be bitter. It would be easy to attack. But the first thing we must do is examine ourselves . . . Because there's something that all of us are not doing right. When our children are pitted against each other at tender ages, when young Black children keep getting buried and young white children keep feeling justified, there's something that we're not doing right. I'm looking at the man in the mirror. It's time for us to change our ways."

—Rev. Al Sharpton at the funeral of
Yusuf Hawkins, August 30, 1989

O N THE HOT and humid Saturday after Labor Day in 1989, three days before primary day in New York, a small group of Black men and women were milling about at Grand Army Plaza in Brooklyn in preparation for a march. It was three weeks after the murder of the young Black man Yusuf Hawkins by a mob of white youths in the Brooklyn neighborhood of Bensonhurst, and the heat of the day was intensified by the stress engendered by the Hawkins slaying. It had been rumored that this march, like earlier ones, would be led by Rev. Al Sharpton. Despite the temperature and the sweltering air, the marchers assembled that morning to walk the five miles through Brooklyn into Bensonhurst to the spot where Yusuf Hawkins was shot. As the hour of departure passed with no sign of Sharpton, a ripple of uncertainty spread through the crowd, and the marchers began to argue among themselves about the wisdom of proceeding. Finally, one young man shouted, "The hell with Sharpton! We're going to Bensonhurst!"

As it turned out, Sharpton was in Chicago with Yusuf Hawkins's father, Moses Stewart, meeting with Black Muslim leader Louis Farrakhan. But that day, walking alongside the marchers, I found myself thinking, like the young Black man who rallied the crowd: "Who needs Al Sharpton?" Is he simply one of those big balloon blow-up clowns brought out by the media during crises to make the brothers look bad? Does the man actually exist anywhere but on the six o'clock news and the front page of the *Post?*

Al Sharpton has, by now, assumed an almost mythological relation to the public consciousness of New York City. He has been a longtime fixture in the news, looming like a harpy in the city's media imagination—decrying racism, police brutality, and injustice throughout the five boroughs, the tristate area, even upstate. In the larger community of whites and assimilated minorities, Sharpton is often considered a nuisance, a gadfly, and a buffoon, even a confidence man. He was thought to have been discredited once and for all by the ignominious collapse of the Tawana Brawley affair, in which a fifteen-year-old Black girl accused multiple white men of abducting and raping her, only to have a grand jury later find that her story was a hoax. That was followed by a seeming death blow of several indictments on income tax charges, grand larceny, and fraud. Yet there he was, Moses Stewart by his side, at the center of the most clear-cut case of racial injustice in the United States in years, and much of New York City, if not the nation, was wondering how it was that Moses

Stewart had decided to turn for help to a man so many people, Black and white, had come to view as a charlatan.

IT WAS THE DAY after David Dinkins's victory over sitting mayor Koch in what had been a bitterly fought Democratic primary, a racially divisive election that at times threatened to plunge the five boroughs into apocalyptic violence, and Dinkins's ascendance in some ways symbolized a passing of the power baton from ethnic Catholics to Blacks. Many had been fearful of what might happen, violence from either side, and yet the city was still there, business as usual, on a fine Wednesday in September. Koch had been disarmed, US Attorney Rudolph Giuliani, the Republican nominee, would perhaps live up to a reputation for fairness and integrity, and it appeared to many people that autumn and the general election might pass, if not with genuine harmony and goodwill, then at least with a minimum of rancor and hostility. But in the Second Avenue silvery glass-and-granite building that houses WLIB, one of two radio stations that serve as nerve centers for the wider Black communities of New York, the ambience was decidedly less sanguine.

Since the day after Yusuf Hawkins's murder, Rev. Al Sharpton had been working with Moses Stewart, and in a bit of late-breaking contretemps, Sharpton and Stewart were reportedly surrendering to the police at one o'clock at LIB—as WLIB is known on the street—on charges of assaulting a female television news reporter during one of the protest marches in Bensonhurst. By 12:45 the WLIB lobby was filled with reporters and a TV crew, anticipating the imminent arrival of the Rev.

Sharpton, accompanied by Stewart and two body-guards, arrived at one o'clock sharp. Wearing a black running suit with red-and-blue trim, he swept off the elevator into the LIB lobby and past several waiting reporters with an authority both deft and swaggering. He scanned the space and the assembled reporters with a quick, fierce glance, then bolted through a door to the office area.

Sharpton is a big man, but not tall. His physical presence is imposing. He moves with sureness and grace. One could imagine him in another life as a fiery nose tackle or fullback, or perhaps a heavyweight boxer like his friend Mike Tyson. He is acutely aware of his surroundings. His face is stony, set in a ferocious poker mask, with a cast of eternal skepticism, his eyebrows permanently arched into "What you gonna do about it?" Around his neck is a bronze medallion of Martin Luther King and a pair of hands clasped in prayer.

After ten minutes, Sharpton emerges from the inner sanctum of the LIB offices. One of his assistants, a young man in bright yellow African-style shirt and pants, asks the press to come outside. Out on the sidewalk Sharpton holds an impromptu press conference: he and Moses Stewart, he says, with a kind of schoolyard dare in his voice, have decided to make the authorities arrest them rather than surrender and give credence to what they feel are spurious and insulting charges. (Among the reporters the word is that the cops "don't plan to give Al the satisfaction.") Sharpton takes in the press with a flick of his eyes, then turns to the cameras and in the same booming voice, slightly modulated now, states emphatically: "To arrest the father of the victim two weeks after his boy is buried exposes the true feelings of the police and Ed Koch! Frank Sinatra [socked] a photographer. They didn't arrest him. Jackie Kennedy beats photographers with her purse. Do they arrest her?"

The interplay between Sharpton and the reporters has taken on the air of ritual drama, with Sharpton orchestrating the event like a policeman directing traffic. He knows most of the reporters and they know him, and many seem bored, as if they've been through this too many times before. Sharpton is at base a rhetorician who works with the grammar of the street and fits it all into the symbols and structures of the print and electronic media. If you ask Sharpton, for the record, why he is marching, he doesn't clear his throat and ruminate on the history of oppression; he glares into the camera and barks, "No justice, no peace!" And the suit from Channel Whatever has his quote and can go back to the office.

Sun shielding their eyes, Sharpton and Stewart defer to each other. "You'll have to ask Moses that," Sharpton says to one question. Or, "Well, I think Reverend Sharpton can speak to that." They have clearly defined roles, and they work as a team. "We will march every Saturday in Bensonhurst until there are thirty people in jail," Sharpton says. "There are only four people in jail now." From a passing bus a young white man yells, "Al, get a job!" and up the street a Dinkins worker with a bullhorn barks, "We thank all New Yorkers for their support!" Here and there a walker pauses to observe the goings-on. "Is that him?" one woman asks incredulously, but most glide on by without even looking.

ALTHOUGH HE IS SURELY guarded, Sharpton has agreed to let me spend time with him after the press conference. We pile into a rented maroon minivan to scout for lunch. He is extremely polite, even solicitous. Sharpton has often been burned by the media, and certainly in some of his dealings he has handed the press fuel. But what is also true is that the press has no context in which to put him. In the van are the reverend's most trusted intimates. The young man in the African garb is introduced as Anthony. Next to him is Reverend Harvey, a childhood friend of Sharpton, a big, gentle man who radiates wariness and strength. Harvey seems to regard Sharpton with an almost parental affection and watchfulness. Next to me, in the rear of the van, is Shawki, centered and still, a Black man of about sixty in a gray suit and a black-and-silver *kufi*.

What is most immediately surprising about these men, including Moses Stewart, who sits next to Sharpton in the middle seat, is their ease and serenity away from the media. Except for Sharpton, they are men of few words; what they do say is deliberate. They remind me of groups of Black men I have always known, men doing something they are sure needs to be done, fixing a car, burying a relative, defending a friend.

At a Pakistani fast-food restaurant on Thirty-Eighth Street, I sit with Reverend Sharpton and Moses Stewart, whom Sharpton calls Freddy in private. Freddy Stewart is an intense man of amazing dignity. He is angry, justifiably angry. His son is dead. "Those boys are home and my boy ain't never coming home," he says. Stewart's fury is cold, even frightening. The thought of his son brutally shot after begging for his life—and the overt, even flagrant lack of public remorse in Bensonhurst—is too much to bear. Moses Stewart believes Al Sharpton is his best chance to keep the rest of us from forgetting his son.

He called Sharpton the morning after it happened. "The reason I went with Sharpton is that I wanted to work with somebody who wasn't in the system. Working within the system is like asking a white man to arrest his brother. Sharpton's reputation and integrity in the community, his ability to get results, speak for themselves." He looks at Sharpton and nods.

The nod speaks volumes.

There are millions of alienated Black New Yorkers and millions more in cities and towns across America. This group is bound by ideology, an ideology increasingly hostile, separatist, and disregarding of white or mainstream culture. This is Sharpton's constituency, and it is outside any regular channels of discourse. Mainstream New York can be mystified or skeptical, these people aren't listening anyway.

"We have our own standards of leadership," Sharpton says. "A lot of Black folks didn't believe Tawana, but they say they admire me for not abandoning her." His voice is utterly serious. "Somebody's got to be in there for the underdog. They—the media, the 'system'—want to control how we think. If you are Black and aware of history, Tawana is eminently believable. If you were me, who would you believe? The white police, the white media, or a young Black girl?" He's animated. "I cast my lot with my people. If I am wrong, then condemn me. That's why the little guy says, 'I might as well be with Sharpton. What's the point of being nice?' Dinkins is supposed to be everything they want, and it still isn't enough. The *New York Times*, the *Daily News*, they all went against him. This shows the racial glasses the media look through. What does this say to the little guy?"

On the way back to LIB, where Sharpton and Stewart are appearing on an afternoon talk show, Sharpton hands a magazine over the van seat, the September issue of *Harper's Bazaar*. He directs my attention to a Macy's/Kenneth Cole shoe ad featuring a photograph of James Brown (in prison since December for charges related to carrying a gun in public, fleeing police, and driving under the influence of drugs), paired with a photograph of a Kenneth Cole keyhole-buckle shoe. The caption reads: "Two Great Things with Sole under Lock and Key." Sharpton is disgusted. "Have you ever seen anything so insulting?"

On the way to the radio station, Sharpton and Stewart stop at the WBLS newsroom to deliver sound bites on the day's events. While Moses Stewart talks, Sharpton scans the Black newspapers the *City Sun* and the *Daily Challenge*.

Near LIB, a drunken white man stops Sharpton with a shouted, "What about Tawana?" Sharpton snaps, "What about her?" and turns away. As we go in, Sharpton turns to me. "You [the media] never ask 'Why?' Why are people putting their lives and careers on the line? Maybe because the system is so bad we have to. This ain't no sociology book. I was raised by my mother, and when I was defending Tawana I was defending Black women."

At LIB, Sharpton is a familiar presence. He compliments one of the women on her beautiful "crown." The show's host, Gary Byrd—something of a trusted folk hero in the Black community, a source of "the real deal"—asks the questions. Stewart speaks first. "The police asked me to be quiet, but the next day there were reporters all over in front of my house, with the address the police had given them. How could I trust the system?"

"Everybody wanted to squash this one," Sharpton says. He talks about the media's treatment of Stewart's family and compares it to the treatment of the family of the victim in the Central Park jogger rape case. "Her family visited her every day and the media didn't hassle them." He winds up the show with a good-natured dis of host Gary Byrd.

Back in the van we roll down the FDR Drive to the bridge and Brooklyn, the men cracking jokes about how fast the Chicago brothers drive on Lake Shore Drive. Sharpton sits back and begins to speak more freely. "White liberals are often as racist as conservatives; they want to control Black leadership. I will work with anyone," Sharpton says, "but they aren't going to call the shots . . . I'm not just fighting for Blacks, I'm fighting for me. I am part of the Black community, so I am fighting for myself. People don't understand that."

On the car radio is WABC's right-wing talk show host Bob Grant, and as we thread our way through the streets of Black Brooklyn, Sharpton carries on a one-way Socratic interrogation of Grant and his idiot chorus. A young woman calls up to talk about racism. Grant bullies her. It's possible to be "prejudiced" without being "racist," he insists. She tries to talk about how if you're Black you can't get a cab. But when Grant figures out she's Black, he hangs up on her. All the while Sharpton is cutting with remarks, and there is much laughter in the van.

I ask him who his favorite ball team is. "Don't have one," he says. I ask about music. "I like James Brown and gospel music. That's all," he says with finality, then, "No one ever asks me those questions." To relax, he reads history, biography, the Bible, and the Koran. "Right now, I'm reading a good series on Marcus Garvey." He says he loves movies, but "I can't go to theaters because too many people know me. I just saw *The Last Temptation of Christ*. I liked that. And I went to the premiere of *Do the Right Thing*. Spike used my name in that." What else does he like? He suddenly remembers, "Oh, and the fights. Because of Don King, I've been to every Tyson fight in Atlantic City. In fact, I blessed the belt the night he unified the title." It later emerges that Don King is the godfather of his children.

We drop Moses Stewart off in East New York before stopping in Brownsville to make a phone call. It takes several tries to find an operating public phone, and while we walk, there are smiles and handshakes all around. People call out, "Reverend!" "Brother Al!" "Albert!" A woman stops her car and rushes up. "Reverend," she says, beaming, "kiss my child, kiss my baby." And he does. He runs into a local community organizer on the corner. They slap palms and exchange phone numbers.

ALFRED CHARLES SHARPTON WAS born not far from Brownsville in East New York in 1954 and raised in the working-poor Black neighborhoods of Brooklyn and Queens.

Except for two years in Augusta, Georgia, during the middle '70s when he managed James Brown's band (Sharpton met the woman who became his wife when he hired her as a backup singer), he has spent his life in the Black neighborhoods of New York City.

Perhaps Al Sharpton can best be understood by an exhibit, a 1971 handbill:

SOUL SAVING
EASTER HOLY WEEK REVIVAL CONDUCTED BY
GOD'S 16-YR.-OLD WONDER BOY PREACHER
MINISTER ALFRED SHARPTON
COME SEE AND HEAR THIS ANOINTED LAMB
OF GOD

Sharpton was four years old when he stood before the congregation and preached his first sermon, "Let Not Your Heart Be Troubled," at the Washington Temple Church of God in Christ in Brooklyn, a Black Pentecostal congregation founded by Bishop Frederick Douglas Washington. By age nine, Sharpton was preaching every week, and he was ordained by Bishop Washington at ten. He graduated from Samuel Tilden High School and attended Brooklyn College for two years, where he concentrated on political science. He was also "on the debating squad."

In many ways Al Sharpton is, simply, an old-time Pentecostal preacher who doesn't seem to give a Brooklyn damn about what other folks think, most especially white folks and assimilated middle-class Blacks. He was born and raised in the Pentecostal church, and much of what he does now can be explained by that tradition. Pentecostal churches are usually organized around one man, a charismatic preacher like Oral Roberts or Jimmy Swaggart. The preachers are very sure of themselves and conduct their business with an air of "If you don't understand, it's okay with us, because you won't understand until you're saved."

As a young boy, Sharpton says, he idolized the Reverend Adam Clayton Powell Jr., then minister of the Abyssinian Baptist Church in Harlem and the city's first

Black city councilman. Elected to Congress in 1944, Powell served eleven terms until he was unseated in a financial scandal in 1967. Sharpton was twelve when Adam Clayton Powell took him to Harlem's Red Rooster for an ice cream soda and introduced him around as "the amazing kid preacher." At about the same time he met Jesse Jackson and began working with Jackson's Operation Breadbasket. He credits his early education in activism to his involvement in the fight against Powell's congressional impeachment. It didn't matter to many Black folks that Powell was in trouble with the law; he was their man, and in 1968 they re-elected him to Congress. Sharpton's now controversial National Youth Movement (NYM) was incorporated during this period, by David Dinkins, of all people. It is one of the ongoing great ironies of Black life that various characters can come together as compatriots for a cause or event, and years or decades later be in vastly different political camps, or even be enemies. Thus, the respectable David Dinkins came to represent hardworking aspirational Black New York, while Sharpton became manifest as a gadfly, albeit sophisticated and powerful in his own right.

Founded by Sharpton in 1971, the NYM ostensibly sought to fight drugs and help Black youths realize their political potential. "Black youth will mobilize a force that must be reckoned with from the White House to the street corner," Sharpton said then. "No longer will articulate Uncle Toms make money off youth programs that produce nothing for Black youths. [We] will either have a viable future or America will have to bear the consequences." There have been accusations that at least $250,000 of NYM's funds are unaccounted for. In February 1988, the New York attorney general's office described NYM records as "a shopping bag" full of receipts that made no sense. The shoddy management of the NYM is the source of much of the heat Sharpton has drawn as of late.

It is after five o'clock, and Sharpton is tired, nodding off in the van on the way home. He lives in a modest apartment in Prospect Heights. From the visible evidence, he is not getting rich off the revolution, though Attorney General Abrams might say otherwise. Two very young daughters rush out to greet him, jumping up and down yelling, "Daddy, Daddy!"

Inside, his study is pure function: bookcases neatly jammed full, boxes and stacks of books on the floor, a carved table that serves as a desk, and two sets of barbells. There are portraits of Dr. King, of Louis Farrakhan, of Sharpton with James Brown, and two blown-up photos of a young Sharpton. One of the books is *Progress and Poverty* by Henry George. Another is *Message to the Blackman* by Elijah Muhammad.

For most of an hour he returns telephone calls, coordinating and dispatching, hectoring and gossiping through three time zones. His energy has returned; he is ebullient and decisive. I am surprised at how hard he laughs. When he finally puts down the phone, he talks about the men he most admires. "Dr. King and Adam Clayton Powell are my two personal heroes. I think Dr. King will be one of the three greatest men of this century. He wasn't a conformist like Whitney Young and Ralph Bunche and them. I wish I could be like him and control my feelings, but I can't. I get mad. I want to fight back."

He shows me personal photos: Muhammad Ali, Eddie Murphy, Jesse Jackson, Sylvester Stallone, Don Johnson, Michael Jackson, Mick Jagger, David Bowie, Mike Tyson . . . all with Rev. Sharpton.

I ask him about James Brown. "In 1972, I met James's oldest son, Teddy, through the NYM. In 1973 Teddy was killed in a car crash, and James 'adopted' me. He said I didn't have a father and he had lost his son. He taught me how to promote a show. Man-to-man, the greatest man I have ever known is James Brown."

As he talks about Brown, Sharpton becomes coolly angry: "If there's one man America owes something to, it's James Brown. He supported Nixon, he went to Vietnam, and when he got in trouble, nobody helped him . . . in one year James went to jail, Motown was sold to white folks, and a white dude won rhythm and blues [at the Grammys] . . . I was upset." He quiets down. "We were riding around Augusta, Georgia, in 1980 listening to a tape. James said, 'When we go see George Bush'—that's the first I knew I was going—'I want you to do something for me. I want you to look like we are father to son.' That's why I got my hair done, and I promised James I'd keep it as long as he lives." He shows me pictures of him visiting James Brown in prison.

Sharpton's wife, Kathy, comes into the room. "This man's from Chicago," he says, "and I'm sure he'd like a nice plate of whatever you've got for dinner." Dinner is quiet, a respite from the long day. The movie *The Wiz* is on the VCR, and Sharpton seems to know the words to every song. Behind him is a poster of Malcolm X peering out a window while holding an M-1 carbine. The caption of the poster reads: "By Any Means Necessary." As we eat, Sharpton offers

me this analysis of the racial culture of New York: "You
see, unlike the South, New York never went through the
movement," he says. "You know Malcolm said, 'New York
is Up South,' and folks down South is one thing, but up
here it's a whole 'nother thing." After dinner, I view a tape
of Sharpton with Rudy Giuliani on the *Today Show*. The
tape is from August 1987, and Sharpton and Giuliani are
amicably discussing ways of fighting crack in the neighborhoods. "You can bet Giuliani don't want Dave [Dinkins] to
get his hands on that," Sharpton says with a mischievous
grin. One of his daughters wanders by, smiles delightedly,
and points at the screen: "Daddy!"

The Slave Theater, on Fulton and Bedford, is one of
the chambers in the heart of Black Brooklyn. The walls
are painted with murals depicting *The Holocaust of the Black
Race*: an African field, the slave journey, and a galaxy of
Black heroes from Frederick Douglass to Jackie Robinson,
an African flag, a prison. The Reverend Sharpton is introduced to chants of "No justice, no peace!" and a standing
ovation. He has changed into a splendid brown suit. "Hug
the person next to you," he begins, "and tell him you love
him. And if they aren't African, turn 'em in to security."
This gets a huge laugh. In ninety seconds he is, frankly,
rocking the house. He tells of a fresh racial incident in Chicago, where policemen are alleged to have turned two Black
youths over to a white mob. He speaks of the recent clashes
in Virginia Beach, of the two Hispanic youths beaten the
previous weekend in Bensonhurst. He rejects talking: "We
want a trial, not a seminar."

He is a masterful speaker, better than either Mario
Cuomo or Jesse Jackson, roughly the ghetto equivalent of

Ronald Reagan. The easiest way to conceive of his stump style is Jesse Jackson on steroids. He speaks extemporaneously for over an hour, a stunning display of secular homiletic pyrotechnics. There is no rhetorical technique he hasn't mastered: irony, facial exaggeration, mock irony, scolding, mimicry, call-and-response. He rouses the crowd to nine or ten standing ovations. These are the techniques of the Black church, and he may be as skilled as Dr. King, but with a street PhD. This is the kind of rhetorical ability that has always been the vehicle to influence in the Black community.

He is specific: Yusuf, Richard Luke, school, jobs. He is not interested in coalitions: "These Negroes [read Dinkins] get downtown and forget about us." He is not interested in compromise: "Them kids in Bensonhurst are going to keep on killing Black folks until they have to pay for it. They don't care who the mayor is. They'll shoot the mayor." He slows down. "None of the media who criticizes us backed him [Dinkins]. The *Times,* the *Post,* they all went the other way. The *Daily News* went for Ravitch, who they knew couldn't win. They ignored the good n----r."

And I wonder, where is David Dinkins tonight? Where are the media? There are no reporters at the Slave finding out what these people think. No TV cameras or suits from Channel 4. And absolutely no white folks. But Sharpton *is* here. After an hour, the audience is laughing so hard they are begging for mercy. "You can't make it in this world, but the crackers got you loving *Another World.*" Then he shifts again, to the teenagers who raised money for Yusuf Hawkins's gravestone and found that it was paid for: "They put the money in the bank for the next one." Here at the Slave,

I find myself thinking of the slave meetings, illegal and deep in the woods, that sustained a people.

Backstage after the rally it's business as usual. Sharpton spends an hour counting the money raised in the offering, talking with community organizers. Sharpton is often characterized as a glory hound, but at this moment in the middle of Bedford-Stuyvesant in the center of Brooklyn, there does not seem to be much glory. One of the people he sees is a young Black man, sixteen or so, who spoke amazingly well earlier at the rally. The young man is dressed in black, topped by a black *kufi* trimmed with silver. His mere presence would frighten many whites and middle-class Blacks, yet the boy is well mannered, even bashful. And he has just quit school. It occurs to me, what other Black politician, except perhaps Jesse Jackson, would this young man sit down with? Who else would he trust with his fears? We are in a dressing room in the rear of the Slave Theater. Outside, generations of Black folk are going to hell in a handbasket, and the basket is on fire. I am looking at this young prince, I am thinking of Yusuf Hawkins, and I am wondering who but Al Sharpton is around to talk him into going back to school. "I'm going to teach you like Adam and them taught me," Sharpton says to the boy.

Junior's on DeKalb is where Rev. Sharpton and his crew meet at the end of a day to kick back and argue about everything from the difference between the brothers from Chicago and the brothers from New York to the long-term life and career prospects of the Reverend Jesse Jackson. There are shouts of "Yo, Sharpton!" and a steam of well-wishers and autograph seekers. The conversation drifts to David Dinkins, and Sharpton says, "He can't protect us. He has to get along with everybody. He has to get along with Jews, with businessmen. He has to make them feel safe. I'm only worried about us."

Alfred is down with the home folks, and he's been there for a very long time. Earlier in the day he said to me, "They try to act like we were *born* at Howard Beach. That's not true." In New York, there is something of a three-level chess game going on: whites vs. middle-class Blacks vs. the rest of the Blacks. Each group has different motives and widely divergent agendas. Sharpton represents a piece of the spectrum refracted through that prism of race and class, and whether you like him or not, whether you think he is a new breed of street insurgent or an outlaw one step ahead of the posse, he does have a following, and *they* seem to think he is the last honest man in New York. And if I were living out in Brownsville, far from Cuomo, Koch, or Dinkins, where Michael Jordan and Bill Cosby exist only in the flickering cathode ray tubes of my fantasies, I might think the same. And I think the Reverend Sharpton thinks he is still saving souls.

Sharpton is from and for those precincts that missed the middle class. East New York, Brownsville, Bedford-Stuyvesant. Even if you disagree with him, even if you don't like him, even if no one is quite sure where the money goes, *even if*, someday, he is proven a crook, an informer, or both, it must be recognized that he is representative of and representing a segment of society that will no longer be ignored. He is a symptom of something going on in his country, something that will consume it from within. His constituents have waited for Abraham Lincoln, for Frederick Douglass, for Booker T. Washington, for Marcus

Garvey, for Franklin Roosevelt, for John Kennedy. They have seen the men they trusted, Malcolm X, Martin Luther King, and Robert Kennedy, murdered. They are not even, any longer, tired. They are *weary*. They are angry. And this time I don't think Jesus is going to be enough.

At Junior's, Sharpton is called away from the table to the phone. It seems there is news of a small riot, teenagers fighting with cops in the seventy-third precinct out in East New York. The last I see of the Reverend, he is hopping into the van with Anthony and Rev. Harvey and driving off into the night.

William F. Buckley in Hell

Like it or not, we are becoming a communist country. That's what's happening, that's what's happening. We are beyond socialism.

—Donald J. Trump, in Phoenix, Arizona, July 24, 2021

These tragedies have reminded us that words matter and that the power of life and death is in the tongue.

—Barry C. Black, Senate Chaplain, January 7, 2021

1.

I CAN'T REMEMBER WHEN I first came across the term "counterfactual." I probably discovered it in the mid-'90s while idly reading about *The X-Files* or trying to understand how the ideas of Harlan Ellison ended up being utilized in *Terminator 2*. Or it might have been from a discussion about what might have happened in our country if Dr. Martin Luther King Jr. and Robert Kennedy had lived beyond 1968 and been able to continue working toward their visions of the future. I particularly enjoyed the speculation of the *Terminator* conjectures: What if you *could* travel back in time and prevent x from happening? What might that mean to y today? What might have changed or become possible? What might have been the new inflection point? And because I believe race is at the ultimate root of so much strife, struggle, and suffering in the United States: *How might social, racial, or political life have been different, and better?*

I have enjoyed thinking about this sort of idea in the years since, whether in literary works like Stephen King's 11/22/63 or H. G. Wells's *The Time Machine*, or in more serious scientific contemplations such as the Grandfather Paradox (known in pop culture because of the *Back to the Future* films), or the proven notion that time moves differently in airplanes and satellites.

When I first discovered that philosophical construct—"Imagine what isn't true, but what *could* have been, what didn't happen but *could* have. Where might we be now if that other possibility had been the case?"—I related it to science fiction and high concept time wasting, things to do on rainy Saturday afternoons. As a more mature reader and thinker, I saw the technique applied any number of places, whether a pop masterpiece like a *Terminator* film or something as decidedly serious and literary as Philip Roth's novel *The Plot Against America*.

Even now I return to that practice with some regularity, pondering the silly: What might the '90s Bulls have accomplished if Michael Jordan hadn't left to play baseball? And the tragic: What might our country have been like if we hadn't entered the Vietnam War in the middle of so much other upheaval in the '60s? Or if we hadn't invaded Iraq when our nation was actually pulling together in the wake of 9/11? I even find myself working with more urgently contemporary questions: What might our country have been like without Roger Ailes and Fox News? What might have been different if Barack Obama had *not* been elected? And, perhaps, with the most salience, what might have happened if Hillary Clinton had won in 2016? Or, to put it another way, what if Joe Biden had been the Democratic nominee? Because beyond the pleasures of speculation, I believe—along with millions of others—that all those turns had something to do with the geography of where we as Americans find ourselves now. It's conceivable that we might have found ourselves in very different societal and political circumstances or, as some say, traveling a different timeline.

Such ruminations have been on my mind almost incessantly since the events of January 6, 2021. I still find it difficult to psychically process what happened that day and what I saw on television: thousands of citizens swarming the steps and halls of our sacred capitol, attacking officers, threatening members of Congress and the vice president, defacing the building that represents our country and democracy more than any other. And my psychic distress at this attempted coup, which is the only term for it, is only magnified by the later egregious attempts of Tucker Carlson and Fox News to sanitize those events by cherry-picking moments of relative quiet out of forty-one thousand hours of security tape.

Ruminating has led me to conclude that there is a definite traceable connection between certain very specific events in the past and the actions of very specific people, and the present near calamity. I find myself pondering a counterfactual that questions what our country might have been like without one man. Or, perhaps more crucially, what might things have been like if that one man had made decisions different from those he made. I wonder how our national life would be different if he had acted in a fashion other than he acted when presented with a moral, metaphysical fork in the road at a moment that in retrospect looms larger and larger in American history. I believe that a different choice *might* have, counterfactually, made a difference for what I would describe as the better. Because I have come to believe there is a straight line leading from what William F. Buckley did in August of 1957 directly to the insurrection of January 6, 2021, a causal line that links everything that happened in between, and everything that has happened since.

2.

FOR SOMEONE BORN IN 1960, I have the usual hazy memories and impressions of William F. Buckley Jr. He was a northeastern Ivy Leaguer with what I assumed were patrician manners. He seemed a model of the American upper crust, much like his ideological opposite John F. Kennedy: rich, glamorous, well educated, and Irish Catholic. But Buckley was obsessed—in an almost exact inverse of JFK and his brother Robert—with the harder right-wing versions of conservative American politics. Like the Kennedys, he was not truly an aristocrat, not a Harriman or a Rockefeller or a Mellon, but rather the lucky son of a buccaneering capitalist. I gathered my false inferences from Buckley's newspaper columns, from glancing perusals of his books, and most of all from disinterested snatches of his appearances on television, whether network late-night and Sunday-morning talk shows, or from his own PBS-based current affairs review, *Firing Line*. He seemed to be everywhere, with a way of looking down his chin at whomever he was talking to and an accent that was unrecognizable but that I, in my midwestern ignorance, understood to be "rich guy from Connecticut."

As I was being raised in a pro-union household in the exurban reaches of the Chicago suburbs, I didn't think he had much to do with me, and he seemed anodyne as I rode my bicycle around in 1972 slapping McGovern for President stickers on mailboxes and telephone poles. And as I got older, at times it even looked as though Buckley was playing a character: the regretful Tory mourning the passing of the ancien régime. From my blinkered and nascent left-wing African American perspective, he was a figure of mirth, someone to mock, a figurehead or symbol of what was passing from American life as people like me—young, savvy, forward-thinking, and engaged in the next stage of evolution or revolution— took our places in the new iteration of our society.

Looking back from 2024, I can laugh at myself and fretfully admit that I could not have been more wrong. William F. Buckley was not an old duffer mourning that which could never return; he was in fact the architect and avatar of *what was to come.*

I have come to understand that Buckley was the single most indispensable creator of movement conservatism, the fortress of backlash against social progress that would increasingly define American society from the mid-1950s through the 2020s. One might say he represented cultural backlash not only in terms of the progress of women and young people, but more acutely, the advances of African Americans. He was at the vanguard of spiritual, material, and strategic forces standing "athwart history and yelling Stop," as he would famously write. Therefore, he was in opposition to everything I considered to be an advance in American society since the New Deal and everything that I, in youthful foolishness, thought inevitable. Think about it: Joe McCarthy, Richard Nixon, Ronald Reagan, the Georges H. W. and W. Bush? Even Donald Trump. If you look carefully behind them, you will find the smirking visage, the evil revenant of William F. Buckley.

Buckley and his allies were against the changes in American society that had been implemented well before the New Deal, perhaps since 1877 and the cataclysmic, dishonorably negotiated end of Reconstruction that gave the presidency to Rutherford B. Hayes. Perhaps Buckley's yearning and nostalgia extended to an era *before* the Civil War. But I didn't know all that when I first stumbled upon this paleoconservative vein of Republican politics. I was an African American, happily ensconced in a loving family, freshly immigrated to the North from Mississippi. I was blind, I think, to much of what was unfolding in our society. I just saw Buckley as an affected old white guy with a funny accent, someone who could be entertaining to watch if only because he so perfectly represented what we Blacks in the time of the Civil Rights Movement—along with feminists, gays, other BIPOC groups, and young people of nearly all groups—were outgrowing and peacefully conquering. Buckley represented a benighted past we believed we were defeating.

At that time in history and my experience, I had no idea of the profound effect he had had on society and politics and its various contexts. And I could not reckon his influence upon my life. I had no idea that he was, in fact, a much more effective and malignant force than I, or anyone around me, could have known, a Beelzebub in a sweater vest. He might have been, I would come to learn, the decisive force in how my life journey as a Black person was experienced and, sometimes, endured.

I was a child, as I thought of it at the time, of the Second Reconstruction, an epoch of momentous change, change that was all for the better. I was a beneficiary of the work of Ida B. Wells, W. E. B. Du Bois, A. Philip Randolph, Eleanor Roosevelt, Dr. Martin Luther King Jr., Bayard Rustin, Fannie Lou Hamer, Malcolm X, Muhammad Ali, my parents, and millions of others, all of whom were settling this thing once and for all. Yes, I was a child of the Second Reconstruction. But because of the effectiveness of William F. Buckley, I would also live to be a middle-aged citizen of the Third Reconstruction.

Maybe Buckley and his allies, all those old white guys—and a few old white women, such as Phyllis Schlafly and Anita Bryant—whom I couldn't help but think of as passé, would have the last laugh. Maybe they understood what America was all along, what America *is*. And maybe, just maybe, they would win. From the right angle—pun intended—there are days when it looks like they did.

3.

As with all stories, to grab ahold of all the dimensions of my obsession with the counterfactual possibilities of William F. Buckley and how he put America on a path that led, directly, to the January 6 insurrection, one must turn to the beginning. The story does not start on November 25, 1925, when William Frank Buckley Jr. was born in New York City, but a generation before, in the person of his father, William F. Buckley Sr.

Buckley Sr., known as Will, was a lawyer and oilman. After a hardscrabble childhood and adolescence in rough-and-tumble southern Texas, he'd educated himself (aided by a proficiency in Spanish and friendship with Catholic clergy) and set upon a path that would lead to him building at least two separate fortunes and a family world for his children that functioned as a sort of Shangri-la of privacy and purpose. The family enjoyed an expansive estate, servants, and privacy, including elite educational and religious tutoring. Buckley Sr. spared no expense on the cultivation of his children, exposing them to tutors who were at the top of their fields and who demanded skilled recitations and debates from the ten children at the family dinner table as they grew into individuals who would leave surprising marks upon the world.

That private paradise of privilege would allow Buckley Jr., known as Bill, to exceed all of his siblings, including James, who would go on to become a United States senator from New York. He would develop a drive and certitude that would carry him to a position of preeminence in American society that is normally only occupied by presidents and the absolute greatest of athletes and entertainers. Buckley Sr. was determined that his children have the education and childhood stability that equipped them not only with religious faith and book smarts but also with confidence and status, training that would grant them footholds in elite eastern society and the wider world.

After high school Buckley Jr. served, fitfully and without distinction, in the army. In 1947, he entered Yale University, where his ascension to the center of American society would begin. At Yale he would become a champion debater, and more importantly, would serve as the editor-in-chief of the *Yale Daily News*, where he began writing regularly and became a counter-countercultural thorn in the side of the academic establishment, while simultaneously reaping and enjoying the fruits of being a comfortably ensconced member of that liberal establishment he was poking. Buckley also joined the legendary secret society Skull and Bones, which not only created a network of the most established alumni of Yale, but also gave him access to mentors and material resources that would buttress his future endeavors.

One of the aspects of Buckley's life that lingers is his ubiquity: he was everywhere, involved with everything and everyone, all at the same time. Buckley's presence was as if Sean Hannity, Charlie Sykes, William Kristol, Steve Forbes, George Will, and a somewhat less wealthy Rupert Murdoch were all, simultaneously, the same person. And as if that were not enough, one might add that Buckley was a sometime political candidate *and* a corporate businessman, vigorously involved in several ventures, including a brief interval spent working with his father at the family firm, and later building his own investment and corporate holdings. He was also a skilled sailor who captained his own boats across the Atlantic, a dedicated husband and father, and a friend capable of astonishing loyalty and generosity, even to those he profoundly disagreed with. He demonstrated a mastery over the conventional measures of success in American life to such an extent that it might be said that he was a sort of less-fun, modern-day Benjamin Franklin-lite in terms of prominence in so many divergent activities. In leaving his stamp on several areas of cultural and political life, he can be said to be one of a very few Americans who decisively shaped twentieth-century history.

Buckley's ubiquity was the intentional manufacture of his father, but Jr. certainly lived up to all the advantages that were bestowed upon him. The question, in retrospect, is whether those accomplishments were the most efficacious use of the talents of one so gifted, and secondly, the best application of those gifts for the growth and maturation of the wider community. How was a person so energetic, gifted, and farsighted so blind and misguided on the most pressing moral issue of his time?

After graduating from Yale in 1951, Buckley joined the CIA, yet another organization where he was able to expand his network and further burrow into the East Coast establishment. His language skills—particularly Spanish—were useful in his work, and during this time he also wrote the book that would set the permanent course of his life and make him a national figure: *God and Man at Yale.* The book expressed Buckley's frustration with the Yale administration and faculty for abandoning the verities of church and history; it was also a polemic excoriating what he felt was the fatally dangerous drift left in American society. This book became, in fact, the template for a genre: the young conservative taking his stand against Babylon. Essentially, Buckley rejected the twentieth-century university. He wanted to ban Yale faculty from teaching the work of, among others, Charles Darwin, John Dewey, and John Maynard Keynes. He felt that the curriculum of the university should reflect the values of "those who paid for it," and that received truth, in the guise of Thomas Jefferson, Adam Smith, and Jesus, was all that mattered. As was probably intended, the book was very controversial—who could possibly criticize Yale, and at such a young age? But in conservative circles, it was a runaway success, albeit one aided and abetted by Will Buckley Sr., who subsidized the publication and marketed it aggressively, to the tune of nearly $20,000, an astronomical amount of money to invest in book sales at the time—it's equivalent to nearly a quarter million dollars today.

After *God and Man at Yale*, Buckley was a conservative celebrity, on his way to the hot center of American politics and ubiquitous fame.

Buckley left the CIA after two years and began working as an editor at the increasingly far-right and anti-Semitic *American Mercury*. His next book project would be both a minor setback and reveal his reactionary bona fides, as he went from criticizing Yale, his alma mater, to challenging the entire federal government and implying that it was riddled and controlled by communists. Buckley decided to write a book defending Senator Joseph McCarthy, who was already in decline from alcoholism and an inability to prove most of his claims of treason within the government, academia, and media. But Buckley fervently believed that McCarthy was on to something, and with his brother-in-law Brent Bozell wrote a long book, *McCarthy and His Enemies: The Record and Its Meaning*, intended to defend him, though not unequivocally: "It's clear that he has been guilty of a number of exaggerations, some of them reckless; and perhaps some of them have unjustly damaged the persons concerned beyond the mere questioning of their loyalty. For these transgressions we have neither the desire to defend him nor the means to do so." But all in all, Buckley and Bozell thought McCarthy had performed a necessary and worthwhile task in rooting out communists from positions of influence. As they wrote: "McCarthyism is a movement around which men of good will and stern morality can close ranks." Buckley, whether sincerely or strategically, began to describe the United States as under siege and falling away from greatness. Everything in our society that was not, in his view, functioning, was not working because of the communists and their active coconspirators *and* because of their naive and unwitting dupes, the liberals.

For Buckley and Bozell's larger purposes, however, the book unfortunately came to press just as McCarthy's person and crusade were imploding. Therefore, the book sold little and was read less. It did, however, reveal something about Buckley, and was to serve as a sort of Rosetta stone for Buckley's future activities and the influence he would wield. In Buckley's suspicions of a communist lurking under every bed, on every street corner, and inside every office, we begin to see the seeds of the contemporary Republican Party careening out of control with the terms "communist" and "socialist" being used as epithets against anyone who has the slightest disagreement with the hard right. As Buckley biographer Carl T. Bogus writes, "Buckley had now positioned himself in a way that would have long-term consequences. He had adopted an attitude that would become increasingly problematic as conservatism rose to power and others less subtle sought to emulate him. And in questioning the patriotism of both President Truman and President Eisenhower (!), even obliquely, he had positioned himself dangerously close to conspiracy theorists and paranoids."

Here is where we begin to see Buckley's machinations spilling forward into January 6, when after decades of name-calling, conspiracy-mongering, and conditioning the hard right to distrust and even hate their fellow citizens there was the insurrection on the Capitol, a combination farce and disaster that still seems impossible to believe and by which Buckley would have been horrified. After *McCarthy and His Enemies*, Buckley's next project, in November 1955, was to start the journal *National Review*. The publication would serve as the platform upon which he would solidify his role as the arbiter of the conservative movement.

National Review was intended to supply a conservative voice that Buckley and his fellow editors felt was missing from the American media, providing, according to their mission statement, "responsible dissent from Liberal orthodoxy." Buckley would edit the journal for almost fifty years, and it came to define him. In many ways, this publishing venture was an extension of *God and Man at Yale*, as it meant to analyze, critique, and even mock the confident East Coast elite (of which, again, Buckley and many of his fellow *Review* editors were comfortable members). The magazine was a potpourri of rhetorical approaches, ranging from the closely argued, deeply researched essays of nationally respected thinkers like Russell Kirk to the proto–John Birch Society ravings of Revilo P. Oliver, who was predicting a second civil war in the mid-'50s and supplying the groundwork for the white supremacist and white nationalist networks and activities we see today.

Buckley seemed to think that a big-tent policy was necessary to garner enough subscribers and donors to maintain a viable enterprise, but working with extremists such as Oliver opened the door to wild-eyed claims and language that would become commonplace to the right wing, as well as a conspiracy mindset that seems to have seduced the contemporary GOP—for example: Donald Trump's labeling of anything that he doesn't like as "communist" and anything he doesn't understand as "socialism." Perhaps in the 1950s, '60s, or even '70s it was not entirely outrageous to write, per Buckley, that "We cannot avoid the fact that the United States is at war against international communism and that McCarthyism is a program of action by those on our land who help the enemy," but it is comical, if not deranged, to take such a position in 2024.

In my view, this sloppiness with language has been to the vast detriment of our country, and Buckley himself is guilty of the most serious transgression committed by a *National Review* writer in an essay that he published in August 1957. The piece constituted the crossing of a Rubicon in American history and rhetoric. It was a moment in which anti-communist hysteria fused with anti-Black hysteria in a fashion that would foster such right-wing furies as the John Birch Society, morphing into anti–civil rights factions, states' rights proponents, the Tea Party, MAGA, and Christian Dominionism. These ideological harpies coalesce in the would-be authoritarianism of Donald Trump and other Republican lesser lights.

4.

IN HIS NOW INFAMOUS essay, "Why the South Must Prevail," the Connecticut-bred, Ivy-educated Buckley used his usual eloquence, built out of near-Lincolnian vocabulary and syntax, to make an argument against Black advancement, very plainly casting his lot with the White Citizens' Councils and the Ku Klux Klan. He couched his arguments in the usual "Blacks aren't ready" rhetoric, without detailing either a plan or definitive criteria for determining how to create that posited readiness. Southern whites were to be the sole arbiters of when Blacks were prepared to participate in society—as if it would ever be in their interest for Blacks to do so, and as if they would not resort to a relentless shape-shifting resistance, which is what they did, and what we see today, with antiwoke campaigns, anti-CRT, and ceaseless assaults on voting rights.

Buckley, for all his supposed gentility and "civilization" (a word he used again and again, as if he were its spokesperson), sided with lynching and intimidation. With Orval Faubus, Lester Maddox, and George Wallace. With bombs and fire hoses. And, ultimately, Donald Trump, Marjorie Taylor Greene, and the partisans of January 6 sided with him. Buckley, years later, would admit that he was wrong, stating that he had misread the situation, that he had spoken tactically, and that he had thought the white South would come around. But his full-throated endorsement of retrograde southern resistance and violence is not easily retracted. He gave ballast to southern enmity at just the time the nation was beginning to confront the epic wrongs of the past and the workaday injustice of the southern way of life. (This is not to say that what was, and is, going on in northern cities could be construed as justice. But there were and are quantitative and qualitative differences in life and social opportunities between North and South, and in the ability of Blacks to exercise their civil rights, including their rights to vote).

Buckley sided with bullies and supremacists: "In some parts of the South, the White community merely intends to prevail—that is all. It means to prevail on any issue on which there is corporate disagreement between Negro and White. The White community will take whatever measures are necessary to make certain that it has its way." And he provided what was upheld as an eloquent moral defense for white dominance:

> What are such issues? Is school integration one? The NAACP and others insist that the Negroes as a unit want integrated schools. Others disagree, contending that most Negroes approve the social separation of the races. What if the NAACP is correct, and the matter comes to a vote in a community in which Negroes predominate? The Negroes would, according to democratic processes, win the election; but that is the kind of situation the White community will not permit . . . the White community is so entitled because, for the time being, it is the advanced race. It is not easy, and it is unpleasant, to adduce statistics evidencing the median cultural superiority of White over Negro: but it is a fact that obtrudes . . . *National Review* believes that the South's premises are correct. If the majority [in this reference, Blacks] wills what is socially atavistic, then to thwart the majority may be, though undemocratic, enlightened . . . sometimes the numerical minority cannot prevail except by violence: then it must determine whether the prevalence of its will is worth the terrible price of violence.

Buckley isn't even attempting to hide his animus. He is firmly asserting that if violence is necessary to keep Blacks in their place, then so be it. *William F. Buckley is sanctioning the justifiable use of social violence in the United States.* It almost makes his justifying the continued segregation of public schools, which is something we see to this day—in both the North and the South—seem quaint.

He goes on to devote a significant number of words to what can only be described as casuistry and sophistry—and this is a moment to remember that Buckley was a collegiate debate champion:

> The axiom on which many of the arguments supporting the original version of the Civil Rights bill were based was Universal Suffrage. Everyone in America is entitled to the vote, period. No right is prior to that, no obligation subordinate to it; from this premise all else proceeds. That, of course, is demagogy. Twenty-year-olds do not generally have the vote, and it is not seriously argued that the difference between 20 and 21-year-olds is the difference between slavery and freedom. The residents of the District of Columbia do not vote: and the population of D.C. increases by geometric proportion. Millions who have the vote do not care to exercise it; millions who have it do not know how to exercise it and do not care to learn. The great majority of the Negroes of the South who do not vote do not care to vote, [he does not state how he knows this] and would not know for what to vote if they could.

Let us take a moment to pause and assess this astonishing arrogance—and that's not praise for racial attitudes in 1957. Buckley is issuing a loud dog whistle backward to the attitudes of 1896's *Plessy v. Ferguson* that supported "separate but equal" racial segregation just as the nation was wrestling with 1954's *Brown v. Board of Education*.

Then he delivers what I imagine he believed was his kill shot: "Overwhelming numbers of White people in the South do not vote. Universal suffrage is not the beginning of wisdom or the beginning of freedom. Reasonable limitations upon the vote are not exclusively the recommendation of tyrants or oligarchists (was Jefferson either?)."

Today, some might argue, with reason, that Jefferson was both. But Buckley apparently thinks he is escaping the accusation of racism by dragging in the millions of white unwashed: "The problem in the South is not how to get the vote for the Negro, but how to equip the Negro—and a great many whites—to cast an enlightened and responsible vote." The inclusion of the "great many whites" is not just nifty rhetoric, however; it is a Palladian window into how the upper reaches of the GOP often, in truth, still view their base.

As he concludes his notorious essay, Buckley offers what he must have viewed as a bouquet of compromise and forward thinking:

> The South confronts one grave moral challenge. It must not exploit the fact of Negro backwardness to preserve the Negro as a servile class. It is tempting and convenient to block the progress of a minority whose services, as menials, are economically useful. Let the South never

permit itself to do this. So long as it is merely asserting the right to impose superior mores for whatever period it takes to effect a genuine cultural equality between the races, and so long as it does so by humane and charitable means, the South is in step with civilization, as is the Congress that permits it to function.

Just so we're clear: He understands the grave responsibility that the "White South" is burdened with given that "White Southerners" are the *only* ones equipped to judge when Blacks have attained their white counterparts' superior "mores." It is a day that, apparently, has not yet arrived, judging by the social and political behavior of many whites from Texas to Virginia.

Though it is certainly tempting, it would be too easy, a shooting of fish in the proverbial barrel, and ungentlemanly, even, to interrogate this editorial line by line. But it still registers a shock. One would like to think that Buckley, the genteel interlocutor of *Firing Line* and thousands of op-ed columns in daily newspapers across America, was better than that. Instead, I would like to modestly propose another counterfactual, an alternative essay that Buckley *might* have written, one that would have illustrated *leadership* rather than affiliation with the mob. It also would have hewed closer to the teachings of Buckley's oft-stated lodestar, Edmund Burke. Burke is important because he is key to many conservative projects across the globe; he is seen as the advocate of right-sized government, a commitment to locale and community, and a devotion to the small things that make life worth living. When I think about Buckley, I often get stuck on this observation from Burke:

"A state without the means of some change is without the means of its conservation." Or, to think of it in terms of physics, there has to be some flexibility in the system. Bend, or you will break.

So, what if Buckley, instead of siding with Faubus at Little Rock, had listened to Eisenhower, who was not necessarily a fan of integration, but who felt it was his duty to follow the instructions of the Supreme Court?

In a counterfactual experiment, what if Buckley had written something like this:

> *My fellow Americans. Here, in 1957, we have come to a cross-roads in the glorious and combustible history of our nation, one in which we must finally determine whether we can live up to the language and promises of our founding documents, and follow the course that our wisest leaders, the members of the Supreme Court, have decided it is now time to follow. Our fellow Americans, the Negroes, have begun to press for their full embodied rights as citizens, and from where I sit, knowing what Negro soldiers have done in World War I, World War II, and the Korean conflict, knowing how they have served in our factories, businesses, and schools, and perhaps most pertinently, in our homes, often sleeping in the same buildings within proximity to us and our children, who they nurture and care for, I now admit I both understand their suit and encourage my fellow whites to accept what is, in my judgment, inevitable.*
>
> *As a nation, we made a mistake fighting the Civil War, with its violent division and creation of what can seem to be unhealable wounds. We made an even greater error by not grasping the opportunity for change that was before us at that time, during what has now come to be known as Reconstruc-*

tion. But this is not the moment for grieving the past. It is the moment for grasping the future, for listening to that greatest American of us all, Abraham Lincoln, who in his Second Inaugural Address admonished us, "With malice toward none, with charity for all, with firmness in the right as God gives us to see the right, let us strive on to finish the work we are in, to bind up the nation's wounds."

It is a time to forgive and reconcile, to heal the damage that the practice of segregation and the repression of Negroes have visited upon our nation. This, of course, is not the work of a few days. It took generations to bring us to this moment, and it will take generations to resolve. But we can begin, and I encourage my fellow citizens, and especially my fellow conservatives, to seize this moment and this opportunity.

We must also be mindful of what we are consigning to our children: have we not spent enough centuries locked in a battle over the ramifications of race in our society? How much longer do we want this to foment? We cannot see the future, and we do not know what the road ahead will bring, but we know what direction we can bequeath to our children, and we can direct them down a path toward reconciliation and harmony, not conflict, division, and violence.

I must underscore: We cannot expect the Negroes to accept that which we ourselves would not accept, and by attempting to continue to dominate them we are dooming our children and grandchildren to an ultimate conflict that will cripple this nation that we love. Negroes have proven themselves in our homes, in our businesses, in our battles. They have been loyal, and, as they have watched us for three hundred years, we cannot expect them to not want that which they have so closely observed.

Finally, my own forebears came to this country from Ireland—they worked their way up from poverty in Texas, using the public university system. My own father became a lawyer and built a company that enabled him to raise our family in comfort and security. In my maturity, I have come to realize that we cannot deny others the processes of betterment of which we have robustly availed ourselves and perennially enjoyed. We must muddle through, however unpleasant the prospect. I do not underestimate the difficulty. But it is our destiny, and it is time to shoulder this crux as the next American frontier and the challenge beyond which lies the next American triumph.

He could have penned something like that. But he didn't.

Like so many white conservatives, when presented with a challenge, William F. Buckley didn't follow his hero Burke's admonition; he didn't search for "a means of some change." He didn't *lead* those he represented. Instead, Buckley embraced the worst impulses of the day. (And let us remember that he was a northerner, born in New York and bred in Connecticut, educated admirably well). Buckley doubled down on racist and white supremacist rhetoric, dressed it up, and encouraged fellow conservatives toward violent resistance. And though in the future he would admit that he had been in error, the die had been cast: Republicans, following the guidance of *National Review*, would embark upon a series of moves that would result in the nomination of Barry Goldwater in 1964 and ultimately the election of Richard Nixon in 1968. Nixon's use of the Southern Strategy, with its deliberate implementation of a racial divide and conquer stratagem, would be the template for the next fifty years of Republican political praxis.

The GOP, right up through the Tea Party and Trumpism, became the party of white Resistance, and Buckley's "Why the South Must Prevail" has lived on as an ideology, the ramifications of which we endure to this day. Yet he never suffered any consequences for these incendiary statements and activities. In fact, he was lionized: he became the William F. Buckley of *Firing Line* and the author of a syndicated column and dozens of books, a fixture of the highest reaches of Manhattan society.

5.

THE QUESTION THAT HAS occupied my thoughts for nearly as long as I have been able to comprehend national politics is why the GOP has chosen to appeal, in a paraphrase of Lincoln, to the lesser angels of their constituents' natures.

Since Nixon's loss in 1960, the Republican Party has pursued, with impunity, a strategy of division and strife rather than one of healing and reconciliation. Even Goldwater's campaign in 1964, which was not as overtly racial as those to come, presented what we would now call "memes" that implied that individual whites' rights were being trampled and that civil rights interfered with property and commercial rights. (Nixon noticed that Goldwater's messages of "states' rights" and "extremism in defense of liberty" resonated profoundly with southern whites, setting the stage for the Southern Strategy). Nixon codified Goldwater's themes into a definitive set of tactics and took them to a national stage; these ideas, along with the "law and order" concerns following the violent chaos of 1968 and the siphoning of some Democratic votes by George Wallace's third-party campaign, enabled Nixon to squeak into the White House. And every four years since then, the GOP has designed and refined some technique to stoke racial division and keep its portion of the electorate angry and motivated.

But what if the GOP had chosen to educate their voters? What if not only William F. Buckley but Nixon, Reagan, and the Bushes had taken *race* out of the equation and talked about finishing the work of Lincoln? What if they had offered more than token plans for Black capitalism? What if Nixon had gone on national television and said, simply, "It is time for this to be over." Instead, on June 11, 1963, John F. Kennedy gave a nationally televised speech in which he said the following:

> The fires of frustration and discord are burning in every city, North and South, where legal remedies are not at hand. Redress is sought in the streets, in demonstrations, parades, and protests which create tensions and threaten violence and threaten lives.
>
> We face, therefore, a moral crisis as a country and as a people. It cannot be met by repressive police action. It cannot be left to increased demonstrations in the streets. It cannot be quieted by token moves or talk. It is a time to act in the Congress, in your State and local legislative body and, above all, in all of our daily lives.
>
> It is not enough to pin the blame on others, to say this is a problem of one section of the country or another, or deplore the fact that we face.

A great change is at hand, and our task, our obligation, is to make that revolution, that change, peaceful
and constructive for all.

Those who do nothing are inviting shame as well
as violence. Those who act boldly are recognizing right
as well as reality.

Now, to think again counterfactually, what if a Republican had given that speech? Might it have registered even
more widely with those who most needed to hear its message?

I have returned repeatedly over the decades to a simple
but unanswered question: why don't Republicans lead and
educate their constituency? I am not so naive as to think
that there will suddenly be an eruption of clear thinking and
fellow feeling on the part of the average racist white person.
But some might begin to see things differently, and some
independents might drift toward the party, and even some
Black conservative Democrats might feel that the GOP was
a more natural fit for their beliefs. After all, who are the most
pragmatically conservative people in the country? I would
say: successful, homeowning, hardworking Black folks.
They tend to be Catholic or evangelical and among the
nation's most dependable churchgoers. They are devoted
to order and predictability. They save and invest, quietly
conduct their business and then go home—*because they have
to be like that.* It's how they make it in America.

But those Black folks are not ignorant. They are not
going to vote or associate with politicians who play footsie
with white supremacists and white nationalists, not to mention garden variety fearful or ignorant white citizens who
are not interested in facing the truth that they are becoming,

sooner than they think, an ever-shrinking minority. If I were a white supremacist under, say, the age of seventy, I'd be worried that I was going to have to depend on a bunch of Black, brown, and other people of color to continue paying the taxes that support my Medicare and Social Security, after I'd done nothing for decades but antagonize them.

Entitlements are only one of many things we do not want racialized. We face, as a nation, challenges that dwarf any seen before—even including the Civil War, WWII, the Spanish flu, and the COVID-19 pandemic. In fact, COVID-19 illustrates what can happen when national crises start to become politicized, which is to say, racialized. How many hundreds of thousands of Americans died who needn't have perished? How many medical professionals and hospital workers have left their vocations? How much bad feeling has been generated, and how much harder is it going to be to act effectively when we face the next pandemic in the next decade, if not next year or next week?

This all comes back to William F. Buckley: a wealthy, supremely well-educated member of the northeastern elite egging on the worst elements of society, the KKK and the White Citizens' Councils, rather than owning up to what was actually needed in 1957 and acting accordingly.

Perhaps he simply thought that conservatives needed to join forces with southern whites in order to capture votes and build an electoral coalition that could defeat the rising liberal consensus. Which they did. But at what cost? Buckley himself said in 2004, at the age of nearly eighty, that he "once believed we could evolve our way out up of Jim Crow. I was wrong: federal intervention was necessary." That was 2004, when his admission of grievous error was far too little, far too late. And it masks all that he did to prevent that evolution, including the promulgation of his views in *National Review* and its featuring of such gleefully avowed racists as James Kilpatrick and Ernest van den Haag in its monthly issues.

Buckley famously said he wanted to stand "athwart history, yelling Stop." My question for him is simple: "Stop what?" Stop Black people from becoming full citizens? Stop society from evolving? Stop change, which is inevitable, even biological? In our world, when things stop changing they die.

6.

We must all obey the great law of change. It is the most powerful law of nature.

—Edmund Burke

"WHY THE SOUTH MUST Prevail" may have been written as a political maneuver to encourage embattled white southerners to see that they had ideological brethren in the North—among members of polite society and big business. In the end, it doesn't matter whether Buckley's support of southern racism was heartfelt or a diabolically tactical effort to build the conservative movement: he provided succor to some of the worst impulses in American society at a time when things had just begun to open and change. At best, what he did was tragic; at worst, he deliberately set the nation on a pernicious course of destruction that may ultimately lead to its collapse. Race lurks in our memories and resentments, even when it is not the explicit cause of societal conflict and ill will. It often causes us to act in irrational, unproductive fashions.

To pose one last counterfactual: What might have happened if Buckley had decided to speak in opposition to white supremacy, or to at least not egg it on? What if he had remembered how Lincoln, who recognized the tragic dilemma the United States found itself in in 1865, urged fellow citizens "with firmness in the right as God gives us to see the right, let us strive on to finish the work that we are in, to bind up the nation's wounds . . . to do all that may achieve and cherish a just and lasting peace among ourselves and with all nations."

How long did Buckley and cronies think Black people could be denied? How long do his ideological descendants think that Blacks will be denied *now*? There was a moment in 1957, shortly after *Brown v. Board of Education*, shortly after the Montgomery Bus Boycott, concurrent with Little Rock, when it appeared that the country might be on the verge of a step forward from the Civil War, redeeming the failure of Reconstruction, overthrowing the evil of Jim Crow. There was a moment in 1957 when there was an opportunity, almost one hundred years after Lincoln and the emancipation and the Civil War, for our nation to begin the hard work of reconstituting itself.

In 1957, there was a sense that something had to give and a president, the larger-than-life war hero Eisenhower, who would grudgingly implement decisions made by a Supreme Court willing to overturn hundreds of years of specious reasoning and veiled white supremacy. But William F. Buckley—firebrand, businessman, genius, and poseur—chose to ignore the counsel of his professed hero Edmund

Burke: "A state without the means of some change is without the means of its conservation." Buckley instead looked backward, to more brutal, less enlightened times, and sought to impose those mores upon a present that was evolving beyond him. He *looked backward*, embracing a history that was collapsing under its own weight and dysfunction, trying to stop what had already happened as Blacks, against all odds, steadily advanced. He set us upon the chaotic, reckless course that so many have followed to this day, which includes the Southern Strategy, the Tea Party, Trumpism, and January 6.

William F. Buckley bequeathed to us, often with snarling glee, these fraught days in which it seems we might be looking at the death throes of democracy. If there is an afterlife, I can only hope that he has met his consequence.

Letter to Jack

DEAR JACK:

Late one afternoon last summer, we sat for several hours in your car in front of my house talking about a spate of recent race-based attacks by whites upon Blacks in Maine towns. These attacks, unexpected and out of character for the state, set you to reading and thinking about what Gunnar Myrdal called the American Dilemma: the inability of the United States to live up to its stated creeds and goals, a failure that has resulted in a never-ending conflict. You had been reading several disturbing books— *The Fire Next Time, Faces at the Bottom of the Well, Chain Reaction, Two Nations, The Promised Land*—and while much of this bad news wasn't really news to you, having grown up in Chicago, you seemed surprised and mystified, even dismayed, by the depth of alienation you were discovering in Black Americans. In particular, you found strange the claim of one writer, Andrew Hacker, that Blacks never, ever, feel at home in the land of their birth. You said this couldn't possibly be true and asked me if I thought it was.

Jack, I am an Illinoisan of African descent by way of Mississippi; you are an Illinoisan too, Irish and Catholic. We're both from the suburbs of Chicago, we both went to Notre Dame, and we both went on to obtain advanced degrees. We both come from ambitious families who didn't settle for what their respective societies had planned for them, your grandfather blazing the trail out of Irish slums of Chicago for your family, my father, from the cotton fields of Mississippi, for mine. We have much in common and are, at times, frighteningly alike. But then there is this thing that permeates the world around us, that drives so much of what we discuss and how we see the world: I am Black, and you are white.

Sometimes I wonder how we can keep this from coming between us. In our workaday friendship it isn't much of an issue, but the fact that we so often end up discussing it is indicative, to me, that racial matters are a bigger issue in our lives—in our nation's life, if not our own—than we might wish to admit. Racism is, in fact, *the* American issue, on which the country will succeed or fail, because so much else is linked to it. But the country seems to move further and further from any true understanding. I want to tell you a story. I was in Miami recently, working as a consultant for a large foundation there, the only Black person in my particular group of seven or eight people. Let me be clear: the people I was working with were consummately professional in our dealings and more than kind; I was enjoying my stay immensely, and my employers had even arranged for me to have a penthouse suite at a swanky hotel on Biscayne Bay. We conducted our business meetings in the same hotel, and this is where, on my fourth morning there, something happened that I will probably never get over. It may illustrate, a little, some of the alienation I'm talking about.

Each morning at nine o'clock we met in a conference room, outside of which there was a buffet with toast, Danish, muffins, orange juice, and coffee. On the morning in question, having already arrived in the meeting room, I stepped back out into the foyer for one last cup of coffee before convening the meeting. While I was pouring my cream and sugar, a security guard (Black) came upon me and said menacingly, "Are you a guest at this hotel?" My instinct was to resist. After all, I was a paying guest, I was clothed in business attire (which made it irritating to watch whites in torn T-shirts and flip-flops stroll in and out unmolested), and I had been walking around in plain sight of the hotel staff for several days. Why this antagonism now?

I said to the guard, with what I hoped was equal menace, "Why are you asking me?"

He said, "It's my job."

I said again, "Why are you asking *me*? What am I doing that would make you think I am not a guest?" We had reached a standoff, and the guard went for his walkie-talkie. I looked back at the door to my conference room and figured at any second one of my colleagues would come out to look for me. I pulled the penthouse key from my pocket and cursed the guard as he walked off.

I tell you this, Jack, because I want to point out some of the nuances that are indicative of how we live, racially speaking, today, and how damaging they are. My altercation with the guard, who I understand is basically trying to feed his family, is the *least* of the troubling issues. What's really disturbing me in retrospect is how that incident colored the rest of my interactions with the whites I was working with. They had absolutely nothing to do with what had just happened, yet I wonder if they noticed how distant I had suddenly become when I walked back into the room. Jack, I was so angry I couldn't see straight for several hours. I didn't want to take it out on these people, but I couldn't help it. They became implicated in the mess. Perhaps that's my failing, but I learned from that incident how shadows are cast upon the most innocuous of exchanges.

On the plane home, I was even more dismayed to realize that while the guard was in fact doing his job, it was a job with a sort of silent and customary racial profiling defined from high within that particular corporation. I had been in Miami, where fear of crime against tourists is endemic, and the most efficient way of maintaining control is to roust all suspicious characters (though I was pained to think of myself as suspicious). I began to think, darkly, that the treatment I received was what the majority wanted and endorsed. I acutely understood the old joke: *What do you call a Black man with a PhD? N----r.*

I'm asking you to imagine it, Jack—having to be apprehensive every time you're in a new place. The reason Blacks always and forever feel different is that the determination of that difference by others is always hanging in the air. It may be malicious, waiting for a hostile opponent to call you *a name*; it may be innocent, even well-meaning "jokes" meant to make everyone "comfortable"; or it may be the going-out-of-the-way to welcome Blacks in social or business situations. The effect is largely the same. The Black person is reminded of his otherness, his difference, his stigma, and it's exhausting, an invention of whites to preserve advantages. Whites have a power, Jack, real and practiced, and they know it: a power to attempt to insult, to humiliate and stigmatize a Black at any moment. It is the only social power some whites have, their own lives being otherwise full of degradation.

The simplest disagreement between a Black and a white can ignite, at any moment, into a racially tinged conflagration fraught with danger for all concerned. What wears you down, Jack, is this unending peril coupled with the gratuitous and petty assaults on your person and character. This is what causes many African Americans to turn inward and regard themselves as a group apart. It also causes them to give up on the possibility of real community. I think most Black children leave their parents' home for school full of hope and fellow feeling, and then are worn down, some quicker than others, by what they experience in the world. This applies as much to well-to-do Lexington as it did to the Cabrini-Green housing project.

Many Blacks just give up on the wider society. This is, I think, one of the key psychological factors inhibiting Black progress out of the ghettos and rural backwaters, but it can also work on the most credentialed and assimilated Blacks. If I perceive, in a silly example, that a waiter is ignoring me or in some other way disdaining me, do I assume that he's busy or that he's racist? You'll say, Jack, that I shouldn't jump to conclusions, but how do I overlook, how can I pretend to forget, all the previous slights and humiliations?

Why should I give him the benefit of the doubt? Why do I have to act in a saintly way that is not expected of him?

You begin to see the prison we Americans are in because of racism: the waiter can't have a bad day, at least not with me, because of all the bad days I've had at the hands of whites in the past.

Another story. When I was a kid, my parents would rent a cabin on Lake Michigan in the Upper Peninsula, near the town of Escanaba. Each vacation generally passed pleasantly. But as I've gotten older, something that happened there has taken on a symbolic meaning for me. That summer I was about ten, and there were several families staying in cabins down the road from us who were all from the same Chicago suburb of Villa Park. I didn't know what Villa Park meant then: working-class Slavs, Italians, Irish from the city escaping urban decline, i.e., Blacks. These people would have a bonfire every night and roast hot dogs and marshmallows and sing camp songs and enjoy the beach. One night they invited my brother and sister and me, and we went to the bonfire and sat for about forty-five minutes, then decided we were cold and wanted to go inside (I also seem to remember some nightly Canadian radio show that we had discovered and didn't want to miss). When we thanked the parents for having us and turned to leave, one of the kids blurted out, "See? You make us invite them, and they don't want to come anyway."

Through the years, this incident has played over and over in my mind, and it is illustrative of what I think the problem is. I don't really know what was driving that little boy's frustration with us—perhaps he just wanted us to stay and become friends—but as a grown man I know what "them" means. It means me. It means my family, my relatives, Black people, people with dark skin. And the fact of that dark skin, in opposition to those with other skin, trumps all other aspects of my personality, my *self*.

My version of that evening in Escanaba now goes something like this: We were the only Black family in the vicinity, and in a well-meaning gesture, the other families didn't want it to seem as though they were ignoring us. We accepted their politeness out of reciprocal politeness, but then our good manners, because of the racial shadow, were seen as a rejection, while their courtesy was seen as patronizing. This is what the shadow of racism does to everything in American life, Jack; it charges everything with a meaning that may or may not be accurate and poisons the most banal of social exchanges. It leads to the current national situation where Blacks are discussed only—*exist* only—in terms of the problems they present for whites.

This estrangement, in both the public and private spheres, is what scares me the most. I suppose the fact that you and I are aware of these issues is itself reason for hope. But it seems to me in the last several years Americans are increasingly unwilling to listen, to *hear* each other, while contemplating these issues. It's as though it takes too much effort to see one another clearly, to talk to each other with precision. We lack a vocabulary. The words we use have been bandied about so much that they are drained of common meaning. They have one meaning for the speaker and a quite different, often contradictory, code for the listener.

A Black says, "Affirmative action." A white says, "Reverse discrimination." Someone else says, "Quotas." Or a

Black says, "Slavery!" A white says, "I wasn't born then." Someone else says, "Ancient history."

This lack of a common language forces ethnic groups to compete, as it were, on an exchange of grievances in which each individual claim cancels all others. These denials preclude any agreement on a common history from which a relevant discussion can be based, and in the clamor, truth is lost.

So Blacks worry that what they view as their historic claim on restitution and justice will be lost if they acknowledge any grievances of whites, while whites feel that they have done their part—or, increasingly, that they had nothing to do with the things that Blacks are complaining about in the first place. It's over. Who cares anymore?

This denial of history's legacy is disturbing. I understand that whites are very tired of all this; that is the blindness of racial privilege. One could say whites don't care, but I think it's more accurate to say they don't care *enough*. Racism and its aftereffects don't affect whites existentially, only as an external inconvenience and annoyances—crime, taxes, calls to conscience—not life-altering complication. When the annoyances get too clamorous, they respond with force: hire more cops, cut welfare, build prisons. But they seem simultaneously to expect some kind of mercy—a magical absolution—to swoop down and end all this. It is, tragically, a mercy that whites as a group have never been willing to grant.

Again we pay the price of historical ignorance. Americans do not have any sense of how much racism has cost the country—morally, spiritually, and economically—and so they misunderstand what it will take to ameliorate it. We can't even speak of healing because the country has never been whole. Is it possible for us, all of us, given the foregoing, to forge a new vision of this country and each other?

Perhaps the problem is that it is in the interest of some to remember and in the interest of others to forget. The immense suffering and dislocations of Africans on this continent are not a myth; to cite and recount them is not to make excuses. Jack, this refusal to confront history is another reason why Blacks feel alienated, because we have our own versions of things, our own memories, which seem to be constantly disputed, ignored, and disparaged.

We have our own cultural windows through which we view the world. Our experience has forced us to. You and I, because you are white and I am Black, can observe the same event, analyze the same pattern of facts, and draw very different conclusions. Consider the recent New York City shooting of a Black undercover policeman by a white patrolman who mistook him for a criminal. Was it a tragic mistake or racist haste? Our social realities force us to be aware of different nuances, perhaps even force us to frame different contexts.

It's interesting to look at the experiences of your tribe, American-Irish Catholics, in comparison with those of American Blacks. Daniel Patrick Moynihan and Nathan Glazer have described life in nineteenth-century American slums like this: "Drunkenness, crime, corruption, discrimination, family disorganization, juvenile delinquency were the routine of that era." In the hundred years since then, Irish Catholics have become the single most successful ethnic group in the country while significant numbers of Blacks fall further and further behind. Why is that,

Jack? Simple industry on the part of the Irish? Black incompetence? Or is it because, whatever else Blacks do—become spiritual WASPs or street criminals—they cannot become white?

When your ancestors arrived in Boston, New York, Chicago, they had a very hard time, but they did get a chance. So did the Germans, Italians, Slavs, Scandinavians, and others who came to America. There were Blacks in Boston, New York, and Chicago then too, and there are many more now, but millions of them have still not gotten a chance at the full possibilities of American life, partially because groups like Irish Catholics have seen them as a threat and suppressed them ruthlessly.

I think of an article I read last year in which an Irish woman in the Mount Greenwood neighborhood of Chicago—a consciously segregated all-white Irish enclave—told a reporter who asked for comment on the unabashed disdain of Blacks the reporter was discovering there: "You don't have to keep bringing up that they were slaves." That struck me. Why? Were Blacks not slaves? Is it not relevant anymore? Does she not want to think of it? While I was contemplating this woman's desire to deny Blacks their history, it also occurred to me that there is no group on this planet that clings more vociferously to the past, to a sense of cosmic injustice and tragic destiny, even while living in places like Lexington, Bronxville, and Kenilworth, than Irish Catholics. So why must Black history be denied?

Something I've learned from our talks, Jack, is that whites have their own myths and ways of seeing themselves, their own narratives of suffering and success, which often do not leave much room for other, competing, concerns. The suffering in the old country and the ideal of boot-strapping one's way out of the American ghettos are what these stories celebrate, and the mythopoeticization of the stories leads to the "Blacks-are-slackers" mindset that infects much of the country. "We did it, why can't they?"

A kind of psychological double knot is applied, involving the invocation of white suffering and then, in turn-of-the-century immigrant groups, the cry of "but-we-weren't-here-anyway." This leads to an interesting point: just as whites need to learn more about Blacks, Blacks need to understand better white legends and perceptions, and how they shape what happens in our society.

In the *New Republic*, political columnist Fred Barnes wrote, "I'm waiting for a politician to say that white racism is one part of the problem, but there's another part, an internal problem in the Black community—crime, gangs, illegitimacy, welfare dependency—that Blacks must confront aggressively." This statement, besides being obvious, is true; but were I able to speak with Mr. Barnes on this subject, I would have a question for him: Where do "white racism" and "internal Black problems" intersect? Might they be connected? To paraphrase Reinhold Niebuhr, can immoral behavior by Blacks be separated from immoral society? Are whites not privileged in our society, and doesn't that privilege work in ways damaging to others? Jack, some will say that I'm making excuses, but I would say I'm merely describing. It's amusing to me that there is such a fervor over multiculturalism and Afrocentrism and the like these days, because whites—after years and years and years of sending signals, overt and implicit, that Blacks are not welcome in American society—seem surprised that some Blacks would want to separate themselves from it. Historically, in every possible legal, cultural, and social way they could, whites have obstructed, undermined, and oppressed Blacks. Whites lock us out, Jack, then chastise us for not coming in. They deign to bring us in, then they complain that we don't know how to act or are ungrateful. They castigate us for not meeting standards they themselves have never met, and they ignore the fact that the problems facing Blacks are the same problems their forebears faced, but without the handicaps imposed on us. And whites couldn't have transcended without the very government they vilify and accuse of throwing money away on Blacks. Didn't the GI Bill, VA mortgages, college loans, Social Security, the interstate highway program, military spending, et al. greatly help whites rise?

When have whites, even grudgingly, accepted Blacks as a group? Why have they designed and acceded to a system that can have only one outcome, then acted astonished when that outcome occurs? That brings us to the saddest part of all: I think that large numbers of Blacks are giving up, turning their backs on any kind of transformative future, settling instead for a kind of internal exile, a permanent state of alienation.

Much of the way the Black and white people of the United States have interacted in the last fifty years has been predicated on the forbearance of the Blacks—being more Christian, more forgiving, more patient, more in good hope than whites. I don't think large numbers of Blacks are concerned with being "better" anymore, Jack, particularly the youth. They're just angry. There comes a time when calm waiting begins to look like begging.

So we retreat. And attack. The time of innocence is past. We lost a tremendous opportunity in this country after the Civil War, and much of our current racial quagmire can be traced to that failure. Americans, Black and white, fumbled another chance in the time of Martin Luther King Jr., and now whites are beginning to shake loose of any feeling or notion of responsibility, or involvement even, in what has happened.

This is to be expected. Being white in America carries its own burdens, and it would take a poet or a saint to see and embrace how Blacks and whites are stuck to each other down through history. I suspect that whites want to be free of this—of *us*—Blacks, and in the current climate that means putting us out of mind. Blacks demand to be remembered and seem to be destined to assume various mythological roles in the national theater: Tiresias, Siren, Minotaur. I think of De Tocqueville: if we cannot be equals, we are doomed to be enemies.

I've painted a bleak picture, Jack, and I hope I'm not saying more, as the Quakers put it, than that which is true. I think I'm speaking the truth, as I see it, because I'm speaking to you, whom I treasure. I have nothing to gain from exaggeration. I don't think that our relationship, or any of the millions like it in the country, invalidates anything that I've said. Instead, our friendship only points to the tragic irony of the American dilemma.

I have to struggle always to remember that a significant number of whites have been very, very good to me; a number of others haven't been so good, but the same could be said of Blacks in my life. I have begun to think that the best advice is to not view humans as anything other than individuals who have the capacity, either way, to continually surprise you.

When we walk out of our private lives, however, we are in a world that is trapped in a false way of seeing people; we are, literally, doomed to our groups, our tribes, and these groups have a way of ending up in conflict. The problem, my friend, is that every single person has to find some way of living through the smoky illusions of race and group, these untruths and lies that fester and pass from generation to generation until they make us actors in a script we didn't write, don't believe, and have no desire to see.

Thurgood Marshall said, "We can run from each other, but we cannot escape each other."

If we cannot find some way to live together peacefully, the alternative can be seen around the world: in Africa, in India, in the Middle East, in Northern Ireland, in Yugoslavia—in short, to commence drawing lines. And when that happens, my buddy, no matter how much we love Notre Dame, jazz, Irish poets, football, or each other, you are going to be over there, and I am going to be over here. And what then?

Prima Facie

*Each of us is several, is many, is a profusion of selves. So
that the self who disdains his surroundings is not the same
as the self who suffers or takes joy in them. In the vast colony
of our being there are many species of people who think and
feel in different ways.*

—Fernando Pessoa

I HAVE OFTEN THOUGHT of myself as having two lives:
my life as a Black man and my other, real life. Since
grammar school I've felt a tension at play in my inner
life, a pull between what was expected of me as a young
Black boy, adolescent, and man, and what I wanted as myself, Anthony. I've been at war, and the stakes of the battle
are who I am and who I can become. When I was younger,
I thought this struggle would end at some point. Now, I realize it won't end, that its roots are as deep as the most fun-
damental problem of philosophy—the uneasy coexistence
of body and soul. As William James writes in *The Principles
of Psychology*, "Our bodies themselves, are they simply ours,
or are they *us*?"

One November night in the early 2000s, I walked along
the pier at the southern tip of Miami Beach with an old
friend from graduate school, a white woman. The evening

was unseasonably warm, and moonlit. We hadn't seen each other in nearly a year, and we were chatting amiably, taking our time. My friend was excited by a book of poems by David Malouf and was exhorting me to read it.

About a third of the way out we passed a middle-aged Black woman who remarked on my friend's considerable beauty and the color of her blond hair. I thought to myself, "How nice," but when I entered the woman's frame of vision, she launched into a tirade. "Oh, I see," she hissed, "one of them who done married a white wife. Think you too good!" She followed us most of the way down the pier for what felt like an excruciating length of time, berating my friend for being with me, excoriating me for treason to the race—then she suddenly turned back and disappeared as abruptly as she had pounced.

I don't know if the woman was deranged or just angry, but the incident wasn't really anything new—this is what troubled me most. That night in Miami was merely one more instance in which I'd offended another person, in this case a Black person, by doing nothing more than living my life.

I can remember conflicts years before with certain Black kids in Aurora, Illinois, one of the towns where I grew up, over my bookishness, my flagrant love of school and the library, and my tendency to make friends outside of the race and to join groups like Little League and Boy Scouts, activities those students considered insufficiently "Black." (I will add that there were other Black kids who cheered me on and were proud of my accomplishments.) One girl was so outraged by my failure to follow her tightly circumscribed ideas of how the Black kids in our neighborhood should act that for two years she and the boys in her clique threw my books in the mud, picked fights with me after school, and threatened a white friend of mine in an attempt to stop us from sharing a locker. In the end, I withdrew from public school and enrolled in a Catholic one.

All along there were conflicts with white kids as well— over the appropriateness of my aspirations and the threat those aspirations posed to them. I wasn't in their group either, and many seemed to think there was only so much achievement to go around. Along the way I also butted heads with Black and white teachers, both groups declaring me too big for my britches, though for different reasons— some whites thinking I was uppity and arrogant, some Blacks thinking I was more brazenly self-confident than was healthy for a young Black.

Most troubling to me were the struggles with my parents, who for a long time disapproved of what they considered my overinvolvement with the arts. *I* wanted to be Martin Scorsese or Al Green; in *their* scenario, I was to be a doctor or lawyer, the crown jewel of our family's long struggle up from slavery. At times my parents seemed heartbroken over our lack of common ground. (The irony is that they didn't project how their pushing me for/toward freedom would lead me to new worlds.) To their thinking, I was courting disaster by turning my back on the way that Black people like them had done things for ages.

Finally, there were the momentary, or ongoing, scrapes with white strangers—the wider world—those people too busy, fearful, or thoughtless to perceive others in any fashion other than as stereotypes. When these people gazed upon me, they saw, in my perception, only what their culture and society had constructed and coded as a "Black man." And a six-foot, two-hundred-twenty-pound one at that. I was a threat to doormen, security guards, and cabdrivers: my mere presence created me as someone suspicious, dangerous, and unworthy of the interactions that might allow them to perceive me as an individual.

Black strangers, sometimes including doormen, security guards, and cabdrivers, and certainly including someone like the woman in Miami, were often just as troubling, expecting me to conform completely to their ideological and cosmological positions, even though we knew nothing about each other.

The problem of defining the self, of authenticity, is a problem for every human being. But for better and worse, it is more sharply and starkly dramatized for American Blacks. (I am aware, and might concede, that some might also think that it is a so-called first-world problem, but we each have to live the lives that we are born to.) Walking down the street, I can't simply be lost in my thoughts, in my (shall we say) soul—in what I'll have for dinner, or a movie I saw the night before, an essay I read—because I'm constantly jolted and reminded, by the looks in strangers' eyes, by their actions subtle or direct, of my *body*, and of the assumptions and expectations that go along with it. What I think of as myself, that soul, is under siege.

A Black man in the first part of the twenty-first century is still regularly being told—by society, by the media, by white behavior and stricture, by other Blacks—what he should think, what his soul's affinities should be, whom he should love and be in love with (and here I am not *only* speaking of race), what and where his ultimate loyalties are.

I have tried to imagine with empathy what the Black woman in Miami thought she saw that evening and why she reacted the way she did. I can forgive her the rage, if not the bad manners. It was almost as if two different zones of reality and history, with their varied expectations of behavior and duty, had collided. To the woman, perhaps my white friend was the symbol of everything that had oppressed her and her people—her family, her gender as a Black woman, her experience as an African American person—down through time. To me, my white friend was merely someone I had sat next to in class, someone I liked / admired / respected (pick one?). I suppose the Black woman and I each had to live up to, and live with, our respective interpretations of the scene, but as Blacks we have historically been expected, I think, to agree with each other—which in this case was impossible.

The desires and intentions others have for me, however profound or superfluous, usually conflict with my own. And so of necessity I devised a way of navigating these treacherous shoals of expectation, a mode of being that allows me to maneuver through society—Black, white, rich, poor—and one that I suspect has cost me something. I learned, quite unconsciously I think, how to be a "Black man," how to slide through the surface of any situation. I developed, in fact, a great many ways of being, a sense of the self as a shape-shifter, a kind of postmodern extrapolation of the "double-consciousness" W. E. B. Du Bois explored in 1897's "Strivings of the Negro People."

In Harlem, talk shit and slap palms; in Winnetka, be the soul of probity; in Mississippi, agree with whoever is talking; with my parents, steer the conversation away from anything remotely controversial. I became like Ralph Ellison's Rinehart, the chameleon of *Invisible Man*: all things to all people, who they wanted, or expected, him to be.

A Black man, if he chooses to enter mainstream society, must manipulate many contexts, must alter his appearance often and change his diction and demeanor as circumstances require. Classically, one way of referring to this in African American life was "bowing and scraping." Today, with a wider range of possibilities in a society that is itself fragmentary and always further fragmenting, the reality is far more complex. A Black man's identity in the boardroom of a bank is different from his identity as an anonymous motorist stopped by the police, and both of those are different from his identity as a husband and father, or, say, with his friends at the barbershop, or at the sports bar. Those friend groups might be Black, white, or Black and white. A day in Los Angeles that might start in South Central could finish in Orange County. How much skill and energy and psychic strength is required to pass, as it were, in those wildly different places? These (and many more) fragments of identity are shifting and overlapping and contradicting one another daily.

Other questions of identity underlie and plague this fluid, protean self. Am I a human first? A male? A Black? A Black male? Or am I a southerner? A midwesterner? After all these years in New England, where I have now lived longer than anywhere else, a Yankee, or a Black Yankee? A college graduate? A bourgeois? A writer? All of those? None?

I think it is safe to say that being Black is not necessarily the irreducible fact of Black people's lives. My parents, and millions of other Blacks like them, thought of themselves as African Americans. They could be fairly described as militantly proud of that fact. But if you had said to them, or many if not most of the other Blacks I grew up with, that they had to choose between their Christianity or Blackness, they would have, I am sure, happily chosen Christianity, even if it meant they would be martyred.

My various modes of moving through and effacing a society, Black and white, that insists self-perception is reactive, not chosen, were conceived as techniques for surviving the resulting fragmentation of self. I now see, as I get older, that the techniques *themselves* are something I have had to survive, as they pose a danger of leading me away from being true to myself, and thus true to others.

The problem, put simply, is one of authenticity—of preserving the capacity for being whole in a specific moment and honest with both one's self and with others.

I HAD BEEN FORCED to consider if somehow I owed it to the woman on the pier in Miami to be strolling that night with a Black woman. This brings me to the question, *Is* there a me that is not defined by others, and not defined solely in opposition to them?

The philosopher Charles Taylor has written, "Being true to myself means being true to my own originality, which is something that only I can articulate and discover. In articulating it, I am also defining myself." Again, I can understand it being argued that this is a first-world problem, but also again, a person must live their life in the place and circumstance in which they find themselves. This includes the dawning realization that not all Black people are the same, nor do they possess identical worldviews, or, dare I say it, identical minds.

Each of us is an original, and as an original has an original way of existing as a human, though we may not ever fully realize it. Emerson emphasized that the soul was a unique and private thing, to be guarded from the world, to be mined, probed, and created in secret. But what does this notion mean to a Black man?

Throughout my life what I've been hearing in various forms is, "Be true to your kind." But I wonder who, exactly, are my kind: the Black kids who, in their ignorance and blight tried to stop me from going to the library, or the old white lady librarian who, without my asking, set aside special books for me on subjects I liked? People who share my epidermal melanin content, and perhaps little else, or those who share my obsessive interests in the interstate highway systems of the Midwest, Glenn Gould, etymological roots in English, Miles Davis, college football, Thelonious Monk, Patrick Mahomes, University of Illinois basketball, and string quartets? Am I my skin color, my gender, my family's social position? Or instead, am I my loyalties, my pleasures, those people, ideas, and things that I love?

How do I choose who I am? How much is society choosing for me, and how much am I choosing for myself? What is the proper balance between those two? Can I be, irreducibly, anything that I do not choose to be?

There are, classically, three constituents of identity—biology, culture, and belief—and the problem in our society is that we turn the categorical (abstractions humans invent in order to assign meaning and hierarchy) into the biological (descriptive facts that cannot be modified and that have an irrevocable impact on one's fate). To describe someone as "Black" or "Irish" or "Cuban" is to say something very different about that person than to describe her as female or left-handed or having heart disease. But we often invest the two kinds of description with equal authority. As Ellison wrote in *Invisible Man*, however, Blackness is not "exactly a matter of a biochemical accident [of] my epidermis. . . . [It] occurs because of a peculiar disposition of the eyes of those with whom I come in contact." This "peculiar disposition," I might add, occurs in the eyes of Blacks as well as whites.

It becomes tempting, taking into account the dangers of imprecise descriptors, to say that there is no such thing as a "Black man," or any of the other socially constructed categories we have become used to declaiming. But we know that this is not quite true.

Again, Charles Taylor: "Our identity is partly shaped by recognition or its absence, often by the *mis*recognition, of others." We form our own identities in dialogue with, and sometimes in opposition to, others. These dialogues can continue in our minds years after the others have lost day-to-day influence over us, as with parents. Perhaps *the* major problem for Black men is that the "dialogue" they have with others in the racist society into which they are born can alter or warp their sense of self at an extremely young age and cause their development as human beings to be channeled in destructive and self-destructive paths.

The Black man, reacting to or against society's image of him, becomes the "gangsta," the sullen servant, the too-friendly coworker whose solicitude carries with it menace—or me: distant, polite, studious, and never there.

WHEN, LATE AT NIGHT, I get on the elevator in the library of the college where I teach, the female student who reacts uncomfortably to my presence as we ride down alone is not necessarily interested in the fact that I am carrying books by Emerson, James Alan McPherson, or Rorty. She may not even be white. And she may be wary of men in general. On my good days, I shrug and say to myself, it's not *me*—not a Black man—that she appears to find so alarming.

When I think of my hours in the library, or in contemplation and in prayer, back when I used to pray, I don't see why my most personal affinities should be of interest, or meaning, to anyone but me and those few with whom I choose to open my self. Why must the people I love, the things and places I treasure, my lifetime's accumulation of an interior life, become subject to other people's politics, shallow rhetoric, and public scrutiny?

We live in a society that forces sincere and law-abiding people to break themselves into little pieces in order to survive it, to inhabit the margins of the culture rather than to embrace it whole. Democracy, in its pure, and even its corrupted form, should allow us to choose a self freely. Instead, in its modern-day American version, it leads, in the end, to a more fragmented self. The tragic legacy of our democracy, as described by Ellison, is that we are freed from sweeping social categories, from fixed, generational identities—and in order to flee the anguish of choice and responsibility, we simply create our own smaller categories and defend them viciously. We are "Asian," "white," "feminist," "conservative,"—a legacy of sound bites, the commodified self, the self bought and sold for its utility.

It is almost structurally impossible for an American—and I stress that I'm speaking for more than Black males here—simultaneously and openly to embrace and enjoy all of the aspects of the culture for which he or she might feel an affinity.

Are we becoming a nation of Rineharts, with different personae at work, at home, at play, at church? Is this the new human condition, what writers as varied as Herman Melville, Walker Percy, Toni Morrison, Richard Ford, Annie Ernaux, Richard Rodriguez, Marilynne Robinson, and Cameron Crowe have been describing? Race, religion, gender, sexual preference, social class, economic power, age—definitions of some aspect of identity are always going to be at odds with others and preclude simple choices.

I am a Black man, however, and I suspect that the question, finally, is not "What does it mean to be a Black man?" but rather, "What is living as a Black man in this society doing to me, to my soul, to my neurological and cardiovascular systems?" *Is* there a me aside from the Black man? Am I finally, and only, my body, or are the soul and body of a Black man two different things?

There is a Zen kōan that says, "Show me your original face: show me the face you had before you were born." But I wonder, can an American Black man in the twenty-first century find that original face under the noise and expectations that surround and overwhelm him once he is in the world? Dare he show it? Can others even see it?

The End of Respectability

1.

IN A MAY 25, 2020, incident that became an infamous and revealing national news story, the science writer Christian Cooper became yet another African American whose life was upended as he performed an otherwise everyday task "while black." Bird-watching in an area of Central Park known as the Ramble—the irony accumulates even before the story is told—Christian Cooper encountered a white woman, Amy Cooper, with her unleashed cocker spaniel in the restricted area of the park, in which it is clearly marked that all dogs must be leashed. Birders often visit the Ramble because it tends to attract ground-dwelling birds: keeping dogs leashed in this area is essential for both the birds that live there and the birders who enjoy watching them. But when Christian Cooper politely asked Amy Cooper (they share a last name but no relation) to leash her dog, she refused and ignored him. Christian Cooper moved to offer the dog a treat, a maneuver bird-watchers employ to spur dog owners into complying with the rules, as owners often do not want anyone interacting with their pets. In response, Amy Cooper warned that she would call the police, telling Christian, "I'm going to tell them there's an African American man threatening my life," as she dialed 911.

Christian Cooper filmed the incident on his cell phone, which allowed this interaction to be reviewed and analyzed by millions of people, globally, after his sister uploaded the video to Twitter. It has become one of the more iconic examples of white citizens' blatant harassment of Black citizens who are trying to enjoy civic spaces or otherwise conduct their lives in a peaceable, legal manner, and it raises questions about what percentage of the American population remains uncomfortable with desegregation and the presence of Black people appearing in traditionally white places or activities. Amy Cooper did in fact call the police on Christian Cooper, telling them that the Black man, standing there in the Ramble with his birding gear and preppy clothes, was "recording me and threatening myself and my dog." Following up on her promise, she also explicitly identified him as "an African American man" three times before and during the course of the call, and begged the dispatcher to "Please, send the cops immediately!" in a theatrically panicked tone, as if she had actual reason to fear for her life. Amy Cooper then put the leash on her dog, which she had been holding by the collar during the call. By the time the cops arrived, both Christian Cooper and Amy Cooper had left the Ramble, but Christian had already forwarded the video to his sister. Later, he shared it himself on Facebook.

In yet another example of what has now become a tragic cliché, Amy Cooper "weaponized" the threat of law enforcement. Rather than simply following the explicit rule and leashing her dog, she attempted to enlist the police in order to retaliate against Christian Cooper for his request that she follow the law. She was willing to endanger his physical safety in a radical escalation and mischaracterization of their encounter to local authorities, although *she* was in the wrong and would be charged with a misdemeanor. She seemed to trust that the police would respond to the exhausting trope of a white female being threatened by the mere presence of a Black man. Why else make it so clear to the 911 operator that she was being endangered by "an African American man"? Why not say she was being threatened by "a bird-watcher" or "a tall man with binoculars"?

Much of the nation was appalled by how Amy Cooper had acted, including her employer, the asset management firm Franklin Templeton, which ultimately fired her from her executive position as an insurance portfolio manager. The situation devolved into the usual American media circus, with much journalistic and television commentary, including Amy Cooper defending herself on a right-wing news show, saying, "I don't know that as a woman alone in a park that I had another option." Amy Cooper seemed to have not registered what millions of others had seen while watching Christian Cooper in televised interviews: he was, very clearly, *a nerd*. A Harvard alumnus ('84), Cooper is a board member of the New York Audubon Society and a writer and editor for science publications and for Marvel Comics. He is exactly the kind of guy who would be out bird-watching on Memorial Day and would want the posted rules followed—not to be a jerk but *in order to protect the birds.*

But what is of greatest interest to me in this incident is something else: Christian Cooper spoke of his concern that Amy Cooper had been punished too harshly, and he declined to participate in the charges brought against her by New York State. "She's already paid a steep price," he told the *New York Times.* "That's not enough of a deterrent to others? Bringing her more misery just seems like piling on." Christian Cooper's gentlemanliness or graciousness in the wake of his ordeal is a premier example of what I would call respectability, or Black folks "going along to get along," extending forgiveness to whites who have mistreated or even harmed or endangered them. Mr. Cooper seemed to feel that Ms. Cooper had already been taught a lesson and that it was in the best interests of society to move on.

The State of New York, at least initially, did not agree. Amy Cooper was charged with the false reporting of an incident and prosecuted for a misdemeanor. If convicted, she could have served up to a year of jail time. The prosecution, however, faced a difficult obstacle: Christian Cooper declined to participate in the judicial proceedings. So, after Ms. Cooper underwent five sessions of therapeutic counseling, focused on racial bias, the New York prosecutor asked the judge to dismiss the charge. "Central Park Karen" was neither tried nor sentenced to jail time. She lost her job and, temporarily, custody of her dog, her treatment of which, in the video, was also alarming.

Yet the potentially existential life-or-death stakes of that incident—of being Black while birding—were brought home to roost that same day: In a horrific magnification of what can happen when Black men encounter law enforcement in otherwise banal circumstances, George Floyd was murdered in Minneapolis, a public execution that was also caught on cell phone camera and transmitted to viewers throughout the world. Millions of people were privy to the nine minutes Floyd spent with his neck pressed under the knee and weight of former police officer Derek Chauvin, the last nine minutes of his life. The May 2024 police killing of Airman Roger Fortson is yet another example of this phenomenon.

In some ways I admire Christian Cooper's kindness and sense of "enough." For much of my own life, I have often come to a similar conclusion. I would have wanted to give Amy Cooper the benefit of the doubt and not destroy her life over her narcissism and foolishness. I might have thought that perhaps she could even have been converted to being an ally, having been shown mercy and the proper way of doing things. After decades of living with and learning about such incidents, my view of such possibilities has altered, and I was glad to see her punished. But I understand—and respect—Christian Cooper's public statement and his declining to assist the New York prosecutor who brought (and then moved to dismiss) the legal charges against her. Cooper is following the spirit of Martin Luther King in gesturing toward forgiveness, Black and white comity, and the gospel of respectability, all of which often involves taking the so-called high road. Since that incident in Central Park, Cooper has written a memoir, *Better Living through Birding: Notes from a Black Man in the Natural World*; he has hosted and produced the popular National Geographic television series, *Extraordinary Birder*; and he has recruited young birders through Feathered Friends, an after-school program he started through the New York City Audubon. In short, Christian Cooper is busy living his best life. Amy Cooper's cruel and dangerous misbehavior is in his rearview.

Fast-forward three years: in the summer of 2023, a similar news story caught my eye. In the Atlanta suburb of Newnan, Georgia, a Black man named Anthony Gibson found himself being questioned and even harassed each time he tried to fish in the lake at the center of the housing development, Springwater Plantation, in which he has been a resident since 2021. These repeated interrogations became so exasperating that Gibson began filming and posting them to TikTok, documenting his unneighborly neighbors, who were disturbed by the presence of the African American fisherman, though they did not seem bothered by the presence of fellow white anglers. "I literally wanted people to see what people like me have to go through when they live in a nice neighborhood, and people don't think they live there," Gibson noted.

His videos began to go viral, and he was astonished to learn that a woman who had been particularly harassing, Tanya Petty, had been fired from her job as a massage therapist at a wellness center. Petty not only harassed Gibson on a daily basis but also called the police on several occasions—again, weaponizing law enforcement—as if she believed that the police would validate her grievance and that she could force Gibson to stay indoors so that she would not have to see him, peaceably fishing at the lake, as residents of that neighborhood are allowed to do. It is not clear why the police have continued to return to Springdale Plantation in response to these spurious reports since Gibson had established his bona fides as both a resident and the holder of a fishing permit. After she lost her job, Petty launched a campaign to get her job back and asked Gibson, through third parties, to forgive her and to talk to her boss.

The respectable thing for Anthony Gibson to do would have been to help Petty get her job back. He might have decided, like Christian Cooper, that she had learned her lesson and offered forgiveness. One can imagine the clip of their handshake or hug making the rounds of TikTok: new best friends, everyone the wiser and full of compassion and understanding. But that isn't what happened. Gibson has declined to help his harasser, stating: "She still hasn't apologized to me. I haven't seen her since." That hard line is, to me, a bit startling, especially from a Black southerner— but I also think Gibson is correct. He should live in the neighborhood and house of his choice and associate with neighbors—white, Black, and other—who wish to associate with him and who show him proper respect and trust. Other neighbors he should ignore as he goes about his life, including the innocuous business of sitting quietly by a pond and fishing, as those neighbors are also free to ignore him, or even resent his presence, so long as they keep their thoughts and opinions to themselves.

2.

THE ORDINARY DIFFICULTIES OF living an American life while Black have been on my mind since the early '80s, if not before. And they have intensified since my siblings and I buried our father, Claude Walton, in early July of 2018.

It was an especially glorious summer day—the sun so bright and the sky so clear it was as if some sort of message was being sent. The indescribably meaningful funeral—he was a Black man born into sharecropping in 1935 in Mississippi— was enhanced by the receipt of his full military honors. A retired army trumpeter, who had been secured by the cemetery manager, a white man, came to play "Taps." (Often at military burials, they now merely play a recording.) The trumpeter, who was also white, had come in full dress uniform on his own time and without recompense to pay my father honor along with the active duty honor guard.

It had been my family's second funeral in a couple of months. My mother, Dorothy, born in 1936 in Depression-era Mississippi had died in early April, and unfortunately, though perhaps appropriately, her funeral took place on a day of drenching rain.

My father's young life had been terribly blighted by his time in Mississippi and his first years in Chicago. After a limited and hardscrabble southern education, he came north during the Great Migration, spurred by the invention of the mechanical cotton picker, which eliminated the labor of millions of Black Americans in the fields. His life did not take a turn for the better until he left Chicago as a sixteen-year-old, lying about his age to join the U.S. Air Force, in which he would serve in both the Korean conflict and in the Strategic Air Command. My mother, who had the benefit in her Mississippi childhood of a large loving family who owned their own farm, felt stifled by the Jim Crow restrictions she encountered there. She had also come north to Chicago, where she and my father met. They got married and stayed married for the rest of their lives, raising a family of three children and, eventually, three grandchildren.

They spent much of their long lives trying to fit into what they imagined was America and to fully assimilate, socially and economically, into the middle class. This was nothing short of an epic undertaking. The state in which they were born was only nominally a part of the United States, Mississippi having seceded in 1861 and never truly accepted the strictures of the nation in the decades since. So, in many ways, my parents were American immigrants when they arrived in Chicago. Yet many immigrants of their vintage from Europe, East Asia, and India would have advantages in the urban North and Midwest that they couldn't imagine and would largely never know of.

Together, they raised their children and held down the same dull jobs for decades in the long-term fidelity to a single business or institution that seems to be receding as a feature in American life. They were pillars of their faith—attending the same church for sixty years—and of their communities. They belonged to fraternal and sororal organizations throughout their lives, serving in various community roles, including as election workers. They became beloved members of their residential neighborhoods, including the final one where they lived in the same house, warmly among white neighbors in a Chicago suburb, for nearly forty years. They brought their three children up to be patriotic, to believe in education, to work hard, and to participate in local sports, clubs, and organizations—as we did.

Claude and Dorothy Walton were models of striving African Americans. Yet when they both died in 2018, they died under the vaudevillian presidency of Donald J. Trump.

This was a tragedy. With all they had given to the country, with how hard they had tried to prove they were good Americans, my parents died under the malicious power and abject postmodern white supremacy of Trump (he plays a subtle game; he dog whistles white supremacists, then he insists he is not a racist, is the least racist person in the world, has lots of black friends and appears with them in public, and so on). My mother never concerned herself much with politics, harboring a mild ambivalence about almost everything except God and family. Mississippi had inflicted too many scars, too early, on her. But my father, even in a nursing home suffering from the dementia that would finish him, knew about Trump and the old attitudes that were reemerging, unjust attitudes and practices that he thought he had long outrun. In his last years, he was heartsick and querulous. Had his striving been for naught?

"What about Obama?" he would ask. And I would think the same thing myself. I would try to engage him: "Well, you know, this is just the backlash from them white folks that were hiding out and jealous." But he found it dispiriting, and in his lucid moments he wondered if his life, his embrace of the mainstream, his openhanded friendship with anyone he met, had been a mistake. I have to say, I couldn't blame him. This was a man who had done every single thing he could, including many years of service in the armed forces, to master middle-class American platitudes and prove that he belonged. You'll forgive me if I survey our country now, riddled with MAGA and Christian nationalism (not to mention the neo-Nazism and white supremacy winkingly supported by Donald Trump), and ask myself: *Yes, what, exactly, was the point of my parents' lives of striving?*

What was the point of all that good behavior and effort to fit in, all that effort to make white people comfortable, all that labor to persuade white America that we were good enough? That unceasing attempt to be *respectable*. Because we thought, if we just tried hard enough, we would be seen as Americans, accepted as Americans. My parents tried to be eminently respectable for eighty years, and what did it get them, in that regard?

In another time, I might have suggested that it doesn't have to be like this, and that with a little more work, a little more effort to see each other clearly, we could begin to heal the racial divide. I don't have that faith anymore. And it's because I start thinking about my father's funeral.

I think about that beautiful day, the carefully orchestrated elements of the memorial service, my father's friends and family all gathered in the cemetery in celebration of his valorous life. And the pointed question that James Baldwin asked comes to mind: "What will happen to all that beauty?" Because I think of all the white people who worked to honor both of my parents at their wakes and funerals. I think about the white people who pulled to the side of the road and turned their lights on, in respect, as the procession passed. I think of the care with which the funeral director made sure the U.S. Air Force seal was on my father's hearse, and that the flag was perfectly draped, with exquisite precision, across the coffin. I think about my father's next-door neighbor, Billy, an HVAC technician, and the moving eulogy he delivered that had everyone in tears. It was all sincere, and it was all love. And I know we have to account for that; I have to remember all that beauty.

And at the same time, I must also reckon with Donald Trump, who at the writing of this essay leads the Republican presidential primary by thirty-four points, even after ninety-one charges and four indictments and all the exposures of his wrongdoing. I have to reckon with how every new revelation of his perpetration of evil and white supremacy only strengthens his political power and unshakeable hold on his base.

I have had to face that Trump is one reaction to Obama from white supremacists, hard and soft, who are enabled by whites who either have other driving agendas (such as corporate benefits, lax taxes, libertarian values, or single issues such as guns or abortion), or who don't care or didn't, in 2016, do their due diligence. Trump is the apotheosis of those whites whose cognitive frameworks were not reformed by the Civil Rights Movement. And it seems there are many more white supremacists than we ever knew. And they could not abide—cannot, will not—what was represented by a Black president or by what was honorably represented in my parents' lives.

But also, quite frankly, people like me let down our guard. We thought after 2008, and certainly after 2012, that we had won—especially the younger people, but also many of us older folks. We thought Dr. King's moral arc of the universe was bending toward us. We fell for the seduction of the triumphal narrative.

When we see, in history's Hegelian reaction, perhaps, larger numbers of whites willing to essentially destroy the country in a fit of pique and racial assertion, Blacks must realize that our national circumstance is not going to be solved by fitting in or being nice. Being nice for four hundred years got those Blacks who tried to assimilate to what was allowed to them in America the phenomenon of Trump and all that came with him, to include the Proud Boys, the Moms for Liberty, Christopher Rufo, the end of affirmative action, and the attempted coup on January 6.

The American dilemma, coalesced around race, may never be solved, and it is now clear that we have not been addressing it effectively. Amelioration, incremental progress, and frequent appeals to better angels have not worked. Conversation has not worked. So, when the honor guard at my father's funeral gravely handed the folded American flag from his coffin to my six-year-old daughter, I couldn't help but be a bit ambivalent. What was it, exactly, that she was being given?

3.

MY PARENTS, AUNTS, UNCLES, and most of the Black adults I grew up with lived under a rubric of what is commonly thought of as "respectability," a commonplace word with so many cumulative associations that perhaps it's a good thing to pause and define what I mean by it before moving forward. *Respectability*, rooted in "respect," is defined by the *Oxford English Dictionary* as "The state, condition, or fact of being respectable, esp. as regards character or social standing." It is then obvious what my parents and millions of other African Americans like them were looking for as they journeyed from the fields to the middle class (and beyond) by way of factories, college and universities, civil service, law enforcement, corporate ladders, medicine, the military, law, and endless other paths to security and at least a modicum of material comfort.

The idea becomes more interesting, and profound, to me after moving my finger down the page of the dictionary and looking at the etymological root: "respect" grows out of the Latin verb *respecere*, "to look back at, regard" and the "act of looking back (or often) at one." The etymology conveys the security—and trust and good feeling—associated with looking at someone in your presence. This is what was so essential to my folks: they pursued a strategy to ensure that they would not be disregarded, derogated, or discounted from others' regard. By this logic, they could—with the power of socially acknowledged personhood—look back at whoever might be looking at them whether that was with love, contempt, hatred, or malice.

To continue, then, with the notion of respectability, we move to a noun, to a state of being, to the possession of, defined by the *New Oxford American Dictionary*, "the quality of being proper, correct, and socially acceptable." *Socially acceptable.* I think this was essential, perhaps the core, of my parents' psychological realities. Having grown up as African Americans in Mississippi, which was ground zero for the systemic abuse and disregard of Blacks, they saw mastering self-presentation and the "rules of the game" as a form of freedom and the only path forward.

It was also, I think, in the African American social context of the past 350 years, a way of managing other people's feelings and emotions and, by extension, their demeanors. It was a form of tiptoeing in order to keep the peace. I think this was both a strategy and a set of tactics, a long-term goal and the individual steps needing to be taken toward that goal, for that generation. Yet respectability was not a new phenomenon: it has been a strategy of a significant number of Blacks perhaps since the time of Phillis Wheatley and Richard Allen, the latter the founder of the African Methodist Episcopal Church in 1816—with that religious body's striving to be respectable embedded and inscribed in its name. Being respectable was a way of not attracting negative attention so that gains could be made with a minimum of opposition. It also had the possible side benefit of allowing Blacks to accrue gains: *capital* (literally and figuratively, fiscally and socially) that future generations would have at their disposal. And in some cases, the hope was, some Blacks would even develop relationships with whites who would come to understand that they were humans worthy of respect and comity. Our children, as Martin Luther King said, would be seen for "the content of their character," and able to fully participate in American society without insult or question. That was the dream King was talking about on August 28, 1963.

The question for me now, and I think for millions of other African Americans, is whether the way my parents chose to live their lives, that unending struggle to participate and assimilate into the mainstream of American life, was wrong.

What does it mean that every African American advance has been met with the near equal fury of backlash, from Little Rock and George Wallace and William F. Buckley to the Southern Strategy to Willie Horton to the Tea Party and to Donald Trump, not to mention MAGA movement leaders, Ron DeSantis, and their open efforts to erase Black history? How were my parents, in their honorable lives, offending anyone? Quite frankly, they weren't, and they went great distances to avoid giving anyone cause for offense. So, if you are African American, you begin to realize that with a significant percentage of whites, *being nice doesn't work*. Or, assuming it ever did, it doesn't work anymore.

Yet it is not like things have not improved in many ways for Blacks in America. And we have seen, in the personal lives of many of us, the ever-expanding social and economic achievements of Blacks; and it is not like things are not going to continue to get incrementally better, at least for a significant portion. But that significant, somewhat assimilated, portion of Black Americans has a large number of legitimate complaints. Further, there is a larger number of Blacks who appear to be locked out of any opportunity to advance—or even gain a preliminary foothold—in America. We see this in the urban North and Southwest, and the rural South. How are those Americans going to be brought into the middle class (assuming they want to be)? And how are the African Americans who have already done their part and achieved going to make sure they maintain their positions when MAGA and others seem determined to undermine and rescind those gains out of resentment?

Everywhere one looks, there are the Tucker Carlsons, the Ron DeSantises, the Enrique Tarrios, the Nick Fuenteses, the Clarence Thomases, and the rest of the MAGA and paleoconservative all-stars, white supremacists, and Christian nationalists who are overtly and covertly devoted to undoing the advances of the last seventy years. For much of my life, until perhaps the 1988 Bush campaign, I had thought that there was a new America, a new Canaan on the verge of realization. But the success of Trump showed me the gross error of my ways. And I am not the only Black American who has been disabused of that mirage.

It is time for African Americans like me, those of us taught to believe in respectability and playing by the rules, to understand that there is a subset of white folks who have come as far as they are going to come with recognizing the earned status and achievement of Blacks in American society. And yes, I am aware that there is a chorus of Black nationalists and Black separatists who might be snickering bitterly at the foolishness of those African Americans who appear to have fallen for the bait-and-switch tactics of white America. But nor can we deny evidence toward the contrary, evidence of whites of good faith, that is also in front of our faces.

Identifying the bad guys is the easy part: those whites who are our opponents have identified themselves, we know who they are, and we can act accordingly. Speaking for myself, I have had enough—as an African American, I think I can speak for many, and say, *We have had enough.*

The problem going forward will be discerning who is of good faith—from the whites we live among, from the whites we know and love, and from the whites we can't quite be certain of because maybe they're indifferent, or maybe they're smart enough to appear inoffensive. How do we African Americans who want to participate in workaday America, or who already find ourselves there, develop a way of living among and with the whites who want to live with and among us, while simultaneously living among those whom we can assume to be our permanent foresworn enemies?

Some of this is generational.

As more of us were educated and economically en-franchised, we began to understand in more granulated, nuanced detail not only what *had* happened but what was happening *now*. We developed concepts and language to discuss it. Some of it is, for people of color, a counterreac-tion to the reaction. Not only are we appalled and angry at the attitude and antics championed by Trump and his followers, we are also shocked and offended at the recep-tion and poor treatment that Barack Obama—an example of the best of us—was given by various organized political forces and the millions of Americans who seemed psycho-logically unable to abide the reality of a Black president.

Young people may already be moving in a direction that will entail a solution. They stand up, they resist. They don't think that being quiet and moving with stealth is the best way to negotiate American racial injustice. They're of-ten described as being "woke" because they are trying to learn how to describe their experience, and as "snowflakes" because they refuse to endure micro- and macro-aggressions that their elders accepted as routine. When I think about why this generational leap in thinking has happened now, I accept that it's not just about the antagonism of Donald Trump and MAGA, and not just of the perennially reani-mated specter of Willie Horton, and not just the Tea Party. I think today's young people had reasonable expectations, post-Obama, that they would be accepted and have ahead of them an open road.

Despite my parents' sincere and legitimate hopes for their children's futures, they also instilled in my generation a sense of lines and limits, a racial craftiness that had to be deployed in order to avoid provoking white wrath and consequence. We knew that even as we became credentialed and successful, there might be problems that would have to be negotiated in order to overcome. By contrast, I think of someone like Alexandria Ocasio-Cortez, born in 1989, raised in the Bronx, attending Boston University, watching Obama's rise. She had reason to believe that the worst of racial conflict and animus had receded as a result of the Civil Rights Movement, Black and Latino advancement, and growing white acceptance—not gone, but in, let's say, a manageable box. Then, BOOM: Trump, the considered and in many cases gleefully avenging choice of tens of millions of Americans. I can imagine AOC and her generation wondering, "Was I wrong? Do I even know my country?" Millennials and Generation Y had been led to believe that racial conflict had largely been solved, only to discover that racism has not only resurged but has taken on new and more insidious forms.

"It is a complex fate to be an American," Henry James wrote, in a very different time and context, but I love the simple eloquence of this hard-nosed truth, James's restraint and understatement. So much of my life is both happily and irrevocably intertwined with white people and people of color other than African Americans. I have quasi-familial relationships with more than a few whites and have since I was a toddler. (I have come to understand that my perspective was shaped by coming from a certain place and time in small-town Northern Illinois, in which racial conflict was not on the front burner. I came to love certain individual white people before I knew there was a war between Blacks and whites. This has been fateful to my life.)

But the truth of my love for some whites does not make my war with other whites any less real. And it does not mean I want to be subsumed into whiteness with a special pass or quasi-white status; I think most of my white friends would tell you that part of what gives our relationships a fizz or frisson is my African American insight and perspective, which blends with their white American insight and perspective to create a third thing, which is mutually enriching and sometimes spectacular. (And when I add the Latinx and Asian American perspectives from friends of those backgrounds and perspectives, I am further enriched and begin to see the fullness of American possibility.) That's the America that I want to live in. That's the America that I want to help build.

4.

SO, AS AN AFRICAN American, I must learn to live with two minds. There is the mind that allows and encourages me to live among those whites, Latinos, and Asians who want to live with me and those I love, and the mind that allows me to understand that I live among whites (and Latinos and Asians and even a few Blacks) who see me primarily as a threat and a problem, who view me as an inauthentic person and a usurper out of place in the United States, the country in which I was born and the nation for which my father risked his life. One way of thinking of this double-mindedness is to return to one of the most famous conceptual frameworks for Black life in North America, W. E. B. Du Bois's notion of African American double-consciousness, which he explained thusly in his 1897 essay "Strivings of the Negro People":

> It is a peculiar sensation, this double-consciousness, this sense of always looking at one's self through the eyes of others, of measuring one's soul by the tape of a world that looks on in amused contempt and pity. One ever feels his two-ness—an American, a Negro; two souls, two thoughts, two unreconciled strivings; two warring ideals in one dark body, whose dogged strength alone keeps it from being torn asunder. The history of the American Negro is the history of this strife—this longing to attain self-conscious manhood, to merge his double self into a better and truer self.

Du Bois's double-consciousness, his articulation of "two warring ideals in one dark body," has informed a large portion of twentieth-century African American life and thought and has been a useful way of understanding some of the psychic and psychological challenges we face. It's also astonishing to me how Du Bois's concept additionally resonates with the idea of respectability, the idea of "looking at oneself through the eyes of others." How do we free ourselves from this reflex, this self-protective orientation toward *others'* views, evolved from African Americans' effort to survive each quarter century's distinct threat to our lives? How do we merge our double selves "into a better and truer self"?

With all due respect and honor to Du Bois, whose contribution to Black life cannot be overstated, I would like to propose that perhaps it is time for us African Americans to recast our conceptual frame.

I believe Black Americans should think in terms of another form of double-consciousness, one that we are going to need to meet the challenge of Trumpism, MAGA, Christian nationalism, and white supremacy. And perhaps Du Bois himself was pointing to the task that I think is currently before us:

> In this merging he wishes neither of the older selves to be lost. He does not wish to Africanize America, for America has too much to teach the world and Africa. He wouldn't bleach his Negro blood in a flood of white Americanism, for he knows that Negro blood has a message for the world. He simply wishes to make it possible for a man to be both a Negro and an American without being cursed and spit upon by his fellows, without having the doors of opportunity closed roughly in his face.

Du Bois asserts that: "Negro blood has a message for the world." What is the content of this letter, you might ask, this missive derived from African American experience? I propose that it is a message equal parts hope and realism, one grounded in African Americans' instinct for self-preservation and overdue liberation from the cognitive chains of thinking of ourselves, first and foremost, in terms of the other and in performative deference to white feeling.

We must live, again, with two minds in the twenty-first century. But this time, we will need a conceptual architecture that accounts for the whites whom we can love, trust, live among, and see as fellow pilgrims on the long road into the American future. (Here, I think of the millions of young and not-so-young whites who participated in the George Floyd protests, including those whites who died during those protests. Perhaps they have also realized the necessity of progressive self-identification and coalition-building across racial lines?) And at the same time, African Americans must also have a second conceptual framework, an operating system, built around the firm knowledge that there is also a subset of whites who refuse to acknowledge our humanity and would have us be, at the very best, second class citizens and permanent subalterns.

What we need is a double-mind that combines Martin Luther King's hopeful vision of "a nation where they [our children] will not be judged by the color of their skin but by the content of their character" with a simultaneous dose of Afropessimism. The latter is an emergent theoretical framework in African American studies (and Critical Race Theory) that posits, as philosopher Frank Wilderson and others note, "a lens of interpretation that accounts for civil society's dependence on anti-black violence—a regime of violence that positions black people as internal enemies of civil society." What I am proposing here is part of an ongoing healing for people of color, an end to debilitating self-consciousness and that noisy presence of an extra cognitive gear that we always have to shift into, one in which we assess ourselves and a situation "as a black man," or as a Latinx person, or as an Asian American, that reflexive, old-fashioned habit of taking into account the sensitivities and opinions of whites before we speak or act. In short, conceiving of ourselves as two simultaneous beings—as Black *and* as American—is self-handicapping because it is exhausting: it robs us of too much emotion and too much time.

If we are to be fully human, African Americans must think only of ourselves and our thoughts and opinions, make only our own assessments and our own assertions, and leave it at that. The end of respectability is deciding to no longer account for or attempt to manage the way I am perceived by others or how others think and feel about me.

We will no longer bow to the soft white supremacy of catering to the racial needs of that subset of white folks who only mean us harm. This will enable hostile racist whites to finally become full racial adults. It will force them to live in a reality that is defined by more than their own thoughts, desires, and perceptions; they will, in fact, have to adjust to *us*, as they adjust to other whites. They will be taught that they can no longer shout us down or stonewall our concerns into silence.

This is of the utmost urgency because Black Americans face challenges that are unique to us at this time: challenges that go beyond the traditional economic and social violence wielded against us—through slavery, Jim Crow, Tulsa, lynching, New Deal exclusion, school segregation (including the refusal to honor the mandated terms of *Brown v. Board of Education*), redlining, the Southern Strategy, and voter suppression, to name but a few. African Americans in the last several years have faced what is perhaps the most brazen attempt to negate Black life since Jim Crow: the attempted construction of an American memory hole (as posited by George Orwell in the novel *1984*) by Ron DeSantis, Christopher Rufo, the State of Oklahoma, and various other GOP bad actors, into which African American history will be deposited, buried, and ultimately forgotten along with the many unmarked graves of slaves.

In some ways this is nothing new. Think of the various aspects of Black history that have had to be excavated, "recovered," and presented in the last fifty years, and which the memory hole activities apparently were aroused by. Yet what we see now *is* something new: an attempt to erase us, to create a national narrative in which our core African American memories and our subjectivities do not exist. These new race games are profoundly indicative of a lack of respect for Black people since denying our history as shaped by our unique American experience is denying our humanity.

As a piece of evidence, I submit:

OKLAHOMA ANTI-1619 BILL
STATE OF OKLAHOMA
2ND SESSION OF THE 58TH LEGISLATURE (2022)
HOUSE BILL 2988 BY: OLSEN
AS INTRODUCED
An Act relating to education; prohibiting the use of
the 1619 Project in certain institutions; prohibiting
teaching certain concepts pertaining to America and
slavery; providing penalties for violation;
preempting field of study; nullifying subsequent
federal action; providing for codification; and
providing an effective date.

Whether one agrees with the conclusions of the now notorious (or heroic, depending on one's point of view) 1619 Project, one would think that banning it from "certain institutions," is a deviation from previous American practice, which would be to analyze and illustrate its failings.

In fairness, this bill did not pass in Oklahoma, but it was filed, and represented an astonishing attempt to prevent teaching about slavery in public schools. The sponsor of the bill, James Olsen, said he wanted to ensure "that our young people are taught our history, properly and in proper context." Olsen was concerned that schoolchildren not be taught that one race was the oppressor.

Perhaps he got the idea from a law that had passed a few weeks earlier, Florida's Stop WOKE (Wrongs to Our Kids and Employees) Act, which, according to the Florida Senate:

> Provides that subjecting individuals to specified concepts under certain circumstances constitutes discrimination based on race, color, sex, or national origin; revising requirements for required instruction on the history of African Americans; requiring the department to prepare and offer certain standards and curriculum; authorizing the department to seek input from a specified organization for certain purposes; prohibits instructional materials reviewers from recommending instructional materials that contain any matter that contradicts certain principles; requires DOE to review school district professional development systems for compliance with certain provisions of law.

It's hard to compile how many ways this is wrong, but I'll point out words like "subjecting," "specified" (who decides?), "certain," "prohibits," and "principles" (whose, exactly?).

Also, lest it slide by, why is it only the history of *African Americans* that is "subject" to these prohibitions? Is the history of Latinx in Florida not of deep interest? Is it alright to teach the truth about how horrifically the Seminoles and other Native American tribes were treated in Florida? Interestingly, a further explication of the act by right-wing Florida language arts teacher Vicki Baggett demanded that the law apply not only to schools, but also to libraries.

The Stop WOKE Act went into effect July 1, 2022.

While I am sure that some of this was just grandstanding by Ron DeSantis in order to gain attention for his presidential aspirations, we must acknowledge just how deranged and unprecedented this legislation is.

When the Black teenagers in Little Rock tried to enter their high school in 1957, they were met by hundreds if not thousands of angry protesting racists, so many that it required the National Guard to force the students' entry. When six-year-old Ruby Bridges was admitted to elementary school in New Orleans, the white parents kept their children at home. But in neither case, nor in any of the thousands of other showdowns (none of which, by the way, can be taught now in Florida since they are classified as WOKE), did any of the worst white supremacists—Orval Faubus, George Wallace, and members of the John Birch Society—say that the history of Blacks could not be taught.

Perhaps the Ron DeSantis wing of white history and knowledge only realized in the last few years that Black people *had* a history—and therefore they needed to silence it. Maybe they were alarmed by those millions of previously mentioned white kids who went out and stood for George Floyd. Whatever the case, it presents Blacks with some hard truths, and it demands of us new strategies. Because again, those white kids were out there protesting Floyd's death, sometimes outnumbering the Black protesters, and they were demanding justice. They were with us. And by "us," I mean African Americans.

Trumpism, in the end, is about far more than race. It is the ugly by-product of globalization, deindustrialization, immigration, climate change, television, social media, the opioid epidemic, herd exhilaration, and more. But its bed-rock is racial antagonism and the post-Obama effort to put Blacks back in their place. As with most social pressures in American history, those who bear the greatest brunt of these changes and dislocations are African Americans in both old and new racial oppressions. And African Americans must adjust our view to counter this reality.

Perhaps the most chilling aspect of Trumpism, to me personally, is the realization that so many whites (Ten per-cent? Twenty percent? Forty percent?) were carrying and con-cealing racial hatred and a desire for revenge against Blacks, immigrants, and members of the LGBTQ community. We are the scapegoat of white grievance, the posited cause for economic failure and social disarray, not the complex global and technological forces reshaping commerce and the econ-omy. Black progress, as embodied in Obama, is intolerable to these people, and we are guilty by virtue of wanting to simply live our best lives. It can be hard to fathom the fuse of rage sparked by the civil rights interregnum of the Second Reconstruction, beginning in the mid-twentieth century. But we Blacks have to survive it and thrive in spite of it. And we can't cut ourselves off from those willing to be with us. (No-tice I did not say "help" us. I said "be with" us.)

I have a specific challenge for the white members of the GOP who are not racist and who want to be given credit for that: Why don't they vocally separate themselves from white supremacy? At the *very* least, act like Mitt Romney, who marched in Black Lives Matter protests, and show public support for African Americans when they can and should. Or take baby steps toward racial seriousness as the Black GOP legislators did while criticizing Ron DeSantis on his ludicrous statements about "the benefits of slavery." I don't often agree with Senator Scott or Congressmen Byron Donalds and John James, who push respectability to parodic extremes, but their rebuttal to DeSantis made me feel like we had *that* in common as African Americans, and that commonality might be a place to start.

5.

THE CONCEPT OF RESPECTABILITY. I should pause and parse carefully what the idea meant to people like my parents, who would have never used the word when describing themselves. And neither would the African Americans I grew up with or, ironically, millions of others who have assiduously sought a path into the American middle class, including whites I have known, loved, and been friends with. I'm thinking particularly of Irish Catholics, who trod their own roads out of British colonialism and religious orthodoxy and mistreatment in the United States, as well as Latinos, Asians, Jews, Italians, Slavs, Arabs, and many other American ethnic groups, often immigrants, often fleeing violence, poverty, war, or persecution in their countries of origin and encountering rough treatment here.

Many of those people, millions of them, embraced the importance of self-respectability. There is a difference between, you see, wanting, defensively, to seem respectable to others who you think might be surveilling and evaluating you as opposed to *self-respect*, putting one's best foot forward so that one can feel good about oneself and see oneself as a worthy participant in the world. Self-respect includes the security of knowing that one has done one's best in any endeavor or circumstance. And further: it implies self-mastery, having control of oneself, not allowing oneself to be provoked into conflict that may come from other places. There is practical virtue and social value in these attributes that cannot be ignored.

Respectability—as *self*-presentation—is a life skill as well as a way of protecting *and* feeling good about oneself. But now I think for African Americans it has to be primarily oriented toward oneself and practiced as a healthy form of pride instead of as a technique for impressing or getting along with white folks. I think of all the African American people I grew up with, teachers, police officers, factory workers, middle managers, and how, whatever their denomination—Baptist, AME, God in Christ, Catholic—they treated *each other* with honor and dignity, often addressing each other with honorifics such as "Mr. Warren," "Miss Estelle," and "Brother Barnes." In earlier iterations of Black life—until very recently, in fact—that pride and dignity was not going to be provided by outsiders or by society itself. So someone like me, who has lived a life of enormous privilege and shelter, must be very careful when criticizing anything that gave African Americans like my parents a means of claiming selfhood and status.

I think of my parents, in their nice house in a prosperous, well-kept middle-class subdivision in suburban

Chicago, proud of their extensive flower and vegetable gardens, their cultivated trees, so happy to sit on the back deck and watch the grass grow. They were beloved by their white neighbors, whose children they helped raise, and who in turn cut their grass and plowed their driveway when they became old and infirm. My parents' self-respect, and the communal respect showed to them, was profound and true, and the latter grew into caretaking and love.

But it is also true that all that respectability didn't save my father from the raw anguish of wondering why—eighty-odd years after his birth in a floorless house without plumbing or electricity in Mississippi, sixty-odd years after his service in the armed forces, fifty-some years after the Civil Rights and Voting Rights Acts—the forty-fifth president of the United States was calling the racists in Virginia "good people." That torchlit parade in Charlottesville, so glibly, scandalously endorsed by President Trump, pierced the veil of my father's late-life dementia and took him back to Mississippi, where he had, as a teenager, witnessed the Klan's lynching of a friend. In my father's last years, some of his most frightening memories of racial violence were reenacted *and endorsed* by the president of his country.

It is no wonder that he died heartsick and confused.

6.

THERE ARE THOSE WHO would describe my thoughts and feelings about the need for an end to respectability as an exercise in "identity politics." I don't know that that is true, but if it is, it certainly doesn't bother me. My smart aleck reply to people who query me in a pejorative way about identity is "when you stop reminding me who and what you think I am I will stop using it as one of the lenses through which I view and construct American social polity."

But I also think there seem to be two visions of America—at least two—and those visions are irreconcilable.

"Identity" and "identity politics" are pressingly salient to this time in American history. Who is more tied to identity than the average MAGA voter? They just don't say so because they think they are *the* identity, the default of the nation, and everyone else is alien. One of the ironies of the end of the era of respectability is that racist whites no longer feel they have to act respectable and hide their racism. They want to—and can and do—let it all out, all their racist antagonism and unbridled id, devil may come. But those folks are going to have to confront themselves with a painful honesty perhaps unprecedented in our nation's history because there is no longer room for such posturing, myth-making, or falsehood. That includes, perhaps most of all, the whites who are not racist. They have had a *de facto* free pass through much of this history and contentiousness; now they are going to have to pick a side. And what *they* decide will determine the next America and how it is built, and what comes after Trump.

As for people of color, if we stop orienting ourselves to superficial respectability, if we stop going-along-to-get-along and trying to protect the psyches and emotions of whites whether they are with us or against us, we might actually start getting some respect. We might start defining rather than being defined by the individuals and institutions that comprise the powers that be. The wider society might stop taking people of color for granted, might think of them as more than "diversity" with which to season and spice their corporations and organizations. They might see us as humans who are integral rather than begrudgingly included.

Most of all, people of color—and Blacks especially—must always remember that we are not the ones who are sick. Donald Trump is sick. Alex Jones is sick. The Proud Boys are sick. Samuel Alito is sick. The GOP representatives in the Alabama state legislature, who ignore direct orders from the Supreme Court (an Alabama tradition), are sick. Coming to understand this, for African Americans and their friends, might be the most important reason that respectability, in terms of impressing or managing problematic white folks, has to end. We have to stop trying to coexist peaceably with people who are insane.

At the same time, for growing numbers of blacks, living *with* whites who want to live with them increasingly entails partnerships, marriages, families, and intimate kinship structures of other kinds. This is good. Yet it is also not without danger because there will be a white reaction, visible and invisible, from those who don't want this evolution. The far right seems incensed by any Black self-assertion and will want to crush it. Republican business magnates such as the Koch brothers, who are not necessarily fire-breathing racists, will take stock of these emerging social trends and political coalitions and figure out how it affects their ability to legislate their own agendas.

But let's weigh all that uncertainty—and growing pains—against losing the Voting Rights Act, against allowing unabated police violence, and against the persistence of sham equity, or what I think of as the bottom-line truth of Fannie Lou Hamer's statement, "We didn't come all this way for no two seats when all of us is tired."

We forget, at our country's peril, those Blacks who have yet to experience the opportunity for education and participation. We cannot allow respectability to lead, in the words of economist Glenn Loury, to a sort of "robust to-kenism," of which Obama was the ultimate example.

If Blacks and all other people of color are to break through to full participation in the life of the nation, then whites will have to be open, for the first time in history, to giving up full control of their power within and gover-nance of mainstream institutions. The much-touted phrase "diversity and inclusion" implies, first, that whites decide who gets to be included, and, second, that they decide how many. The clearest example of this at the moment is the fight over admission to elite universities in its many guises. Inequality is also an aspect of this because the only way out of the inequality is to equitably grow the economic pie: we are in a political situation in which any growth of the pie is gobbled by the billionaire class, preventing growth from contributing to the economic emancipation of peo-ple of color (and less-advantaged whites) and the rebuilding of the country's physical and social infrastructure. Or, in other words, however much the pie grows, those at the top just cut themselves an ever-larger piece, expecting the rest of us to accept the crumbs.

I believe very strongly in the power of the truth. In racial matters, it is evident that we are a mulatto / mestizo culture and that all attempts at purity and essentialism are not only wrongheaded but futile. We are the nation of Santana, Prince, and Madonna, not of the Racial Holy

War and the Five Percent Nation. We should admit and embrace our cultural hybridity and, in the words of the great poet Seamus Heaney, "let that be an image and symbol adequate to our predicament."

While we're at it, we should also put away the old Black respectable myth that we'll work twice as hard to get half as far. That admits to Black inferiority. It again yields to soft white supremacy. No one should have to work twice as hard. We shouldn't romanticize that. It may have been true in the past, but it is the sort of thing that ending respectability should address. No one should have to distort themselves in such a debilitating fashion. We're human, and we should get an honest day's wages for an honest day's work. In a way, this goes to Du Bois-ian double-consciousness: Blacks and other people of color being overdetermined by their awareness of what white people think, want, and demand of BIPOC. In the past, Blacks have often answered these demands in the hopes that respectability would prevail. But that is an acquiescence to soft white supremacy. And as we now see, it doesn't work anyway.

Which brings me back to the cemetery in 2018, walking from the burial after my father's funeral. I walked alongside my daughter with my arm around her shoulder as she clutched the folded flag from his coffin to her chest. She was so sad to lose him and so proud that he had been recognized. When would I tell her my version of the truth, what I thought and felt about the country her grandfather had served with honor and that she, a young child full of patriotism and hope, loved and was proud of? Should I not tell her anything? The only answer I could even imagine was "not today." And not anytime soon. But I knew, and was as a result made even more sad than I already was, that that day was coming.

7.

ORDINARILY, IN AN ESSAY of this kind, this is the moment, working toward a concluding peroration, at which I would normally pause, compose myself, and finish with an earnest, hushed, but heartfelt declaration asking that "all Americans give grave contemplation to the moral and spiritual health of our nation and realize that we are one and need to come together to preserve our union." I would plead for the possible future, and caution about how much we all have to lose.

But I don't do that anymore. That would be respectable. And, among other things, I know that a fair portion of white Americans wouldn't care anyway. They will not accept Blacks, even those like my parents who enact every possible dimension of respectability. They want something altogether different for their Black neighbors—including their exclusion from the neighborhood that is the nation. A sizable portion of white Americans are committed to Black degradation; to Black segregation from civic spaces, communal spaces, and halls of power; and to Blacks' continued economic and political subjugation.

I am working very hard to think about how to separate and address whites of good faith—fellow humans whom I know and love and have shared my life with, gladly—the white people that I know from my personal experiences who want a better and more just United States, the white people who love and cherish African Americans and other people of color. Yes, I have to distinguish my white loved ones from those whites who are addicted to the old ways, whose numbers are larger than my generation ever imagined. I must declare my enmity with those whites who will fight for and insist on what can only be called white supremacy until the nation collapses from the weight of its hatred and implausibility.

I don't want, anymore, to ask—and I especially do not want to *beg*—white racists for anything, whether they are in the street wrapped in Confederate flags, living quietly in segregated neighborhoods and towns, or living next door to me. I particularly don't want to be respectable and make nice and protect the supremacists from any Black person's sincere emotions any longer. And I do not want to perform the labor, either, of managing or protecting white supremacists from their own feelings. It's time for them to experience the mental storms that I and millions of others experience every day, the storms that come from the truth of our American experience. And I certainly do not want to bequeath that labor to my child, or any other Black child as they grow and move into their adult experience. I want that *over* for them, as much and in any way possible.

So, white Americans who have Black people in their lives or who regard us with no ill will, I ask that you do more, try harder, think harder, and separate yourselves from MAGA to stand with me and those millions of people of color who, with you on our side, constitute the majority of the country. And to the others, the alt-right, the Trump-lovers, the antimiscegenationists, the Christian nationalists who think you are inheriting the dominion of heaven, the capitalists who put mammon ahead of the health of their nation by supporting all of the foregoing, I say it's up to you: the future will be as majestic and full of possibility or as bloody, haunted, and full of heartbreak as you want it to be.

To my African American beloveds, I will say that we have to keep doing what we have been doing: telling our stories, moving forward, asserting our realities, and if this is not popular or provokes backlash with some, so be it. Being quiet and trusting that cooperation and time will solve our breaches and traumas has been decisively proven wrong. What we found was that the merest assertion of racial pride, no matter how mild, or the greatest triumph earned by playing by the rules, no matter how fairly won, set off backlashes among subsets of whites that were insurmountable. The game's always been fixed. Consider the frenzy created by NFL players kneeling before games, protests that the commissioner and others belatedly admitted had been justified; the league itself subsequently took measures toward the support of racial and social justice. Consider the current frenzy over "critical race theory." Putting aside that it was never taught to school children, are Black people, in Ron DeSantis's fever dream, to be no longer allowed to develop analysis and interpretations of our own experience?

We have learned that too many whites can only manage the idea of race in our society so long as they don't have to be reminded of it, so long as they can maintain a soft white supremacy of imposed silence that allows them to preserve the psychological comfort of social dominance and the illusion that they will perpetually be in charge and wield the greatest shares of economic, social, and political power—anything less seems to be psychically intolerable to them.

So part of ending respectability is to understand that we Blacks can no longer participate in that silence and psychic accommodation. We must enjoin groups of whites who are thoughtful and open to Black concerns and initiatives to come along but under a new contract: one that no longer privileges white psychic stability and emotional comfort. Whites will have to adjust to and endure what the poet Wallace Stevens, late in life, called a "new knowledge of reality." As will African Americans.

We—Blacks—and our allies and loved ones must speak clearly, and accept and oppose the backlash that will come. We must keep reminding white supremacists and Trumpists that we are here, that we are not going anywhere, and that we insist upon being equal and full Americans. We have to remind them that the conflict they are drifting toward—the first skirmish of which may have been on January 6, 2021—will not result in the victory they desire. No one ethnicity or ethos will, without grave danger to and the possible destruction of the nation, silence those perceived to be "the other."

And in truth, such violence and destruction of spirit and soul, with tens of millions of combatants on either side, would probably, literally, never end. It would almost certainly result in an America that was not worth it for anyone—white or Black, Latino, Asian, or Native American—to possess. This is, I think, a reasonable fear, but also further evidence of the true dimensions of the problem: we African Americans tailored our behavior to the needs and expectations of those who believed they owned us, who believed they were more than us for hundreds of years—and it was not enough.

After Obama

WHENEVER IN THE weeks and months leading up toward January 20, 2017, that I thought about Barack Obama stepping down from office as president of the United States and passing, as it were, the keys to the most powerful office in the world to whomever was the next president, I imagined the event as Obama stepping to a podium and closing a book, as if a long story had finally come to an end: the book contained the story of the struggle of African Americans to gain full purchase as citizens in the country where they were born, lived, and died, a story that had ended with a victory in our battle to gain an honored place at the very center of American life.

When Obama finished his term, I thought one push of African Americans—and as such, because Blacks are *so* deeply entwined in the history and daily life of the country, the nation as a whole—would have come to a close. The story of that push began in Virginia in 1619 with the advent of Black slavery in Jamestown; it continued through the revolution and the establishment of the United States as a separate nation, on through the bloodletting of the Civil War and Reconstruction, to the moral apotheosis of the twentieth century and the Civil Rights Movement. It was a story embodied in the lives of some of the men and women who led the fight—Richard Allen, David Walker, Frederick Douglass, Sojourner Truth, Harriet Tubman, Booker T. Washington, W. E. B. Du Bois, Ida B. Wells, A. Philip Randolph, Fannie Lou Hamer, Malcolm X, and now, finally, Barack Obama.

In what seemed to be a confirmation of the gains wrought by the Civil Rights Movement and its preeminent leader Martin Luther King, there was the inauguration of a Black president, elected twice, that was thought to indicate a kind of acceptance and accomplishment of Blacks. That a Black man could be elected president of the United States was unimaginable until, suddenly, it wasn't. That it happened twice made it seem as if the narrative of Black struggle had reached a triumphant climax, that all the faith and pain and sacrifice had been redeemed, and that America, so often wrestling with the facts and contradictions of its history, customs, and realities, could stretch and change and renew itself. There was a great deal left to be done, but it was a cause for celebration.

It was. It still is.

But the story that ends with Obama also has an epilogue that might actually be the painful introduction of another tale: one that will relate the bitter knowledge that the four hundred years of struggle and aspiration was not enough, that the nation is still susceptible to certain strands of violent emotion and vulgar irrationality, and that too many citizens are still willing to indulge in and encourage, out of what seems to be ignorance and nihilism as well as simple anger and meanness, mindlessly stoking fires of social conflict and disarray in a fashion that could flare beyond society's ability to control or extinguish it.

A DISCLOSURE: I AM African American. I'm proud to be so, and as yet would not have had it any other way, though there are days when I resent the unearned and unrequested baggage such an identity can require. But I am proud of my family, my forebears, and as such proud of, to use the vernacular, *my people*, a people who have stood up to persecution and violence—sanctioned and unsanctioned—endured, and come through with integrity, humanity, and honor. I do not, however, presume to speak for any African American other than myself. I have come to a painful belief that in America, in the end, every Black man and every Black woman, like every other citizen, fights his or her own war. We African Americans can sometimes come together to work on specific problems, but I believe it is naive in the extreme to assume or presume that all African Americans see things through the same lens or will come to the same conclusion of how to react to a particular issue.

To step sideways and emphasize another layer of my identity—the deliberately mixed metaphor emphasizes the complexity of the mental frames under description—these days, I think that we *Americans* (by which I mean all citizens of every group and/or identity) are at this

moment of social strain suffering from an absence of nu-
ance and from overgeneralization as a way of accounting
for all of the legitimate differences and layers of experience we live with: every story about race in the United States is a different story, including those involving
whites. And we tell each other and ourselves stories in order to understand each other and ourselves. But an underground struggle for primacy has erupted, as though a long-
suffering family was fighting to claim the title of which
member was *most* sinned against. And the subjective nature of such claims, which often seems obvious to a particular person or group, short circuits any understanding.
And without understanding, what?

It had been my hope, with the 2008 election of Barack
Obama, that we Americans had bought some time. That
we might outrun history or, to put it another way, fate.
That the United States could continue on its bumpy slide
toward something I'd come to think of as "racial normalcy,"
a new status quo that would reflect current (looming) demographic realities and that would allow for a more peaceful
transition to the coming demographic change—certainly
by the 2040s—when, as in the state of California currently,
whites are less than 50 percent of the population, or just
another group, albeit a large one and one endowed with
considerable economic power. That whites could see that
circumstance as the natural evolving next phase of the nation, and continue accordingly.

I'd hoped that we as a nation could continue grind-
ing toward that new racial configuration, which I was well
aware would not occur overnight, but which I thought
and hoped would generate balance and predictability and

also wouldn't get too out of control in any one direction. And I'd thought that Obama's presidency could mark a huge moment in African American (and therefore American) history, a beginning of routinization in the African American presence here, a marker in the progress of African Americans to "just another group" in the mosaic. And I'd hoped that if African Americans could achieve this place in a new society, then by default every other group that finds itself taking a turn as the scapegoated outsider in 2010s and 2020s political rhetoric—Latino immigrants, Muslims, LGBTQ—might also gain a normalized presence. Again, I didn't expect this next status quo to emerge tomorrow, but I thought that it was well underway and would progress generationally, as it had in the past.

Now, I'm not so sure. But that's who I am, and what I had thought, and what I had hoped for. Until November 8, 2016.

There is an irony, both tragic and celebratory, at the heart of our society: young people of color grow up hearing about the Declaration of Independence and the Constitution, and *they believe it.* They want to hold the nation to its promises, they want to belong and be Americans, free and equal, as they understand those terms, which is to say, in the simplest iterations. And every generation understands the promises of our founding documents a little more intensely, and they insist a little more on the full implementation of those promises. This is, I think, what lies behind Black Lives Matter and many of the other protests that we see enacted around the nation. In another country, one that has not made such promises, there would not necessarily be such a sense of failure. Black Lives Matter protestors, who seem to have struck a profound and deep nerve with many whites who oppose them, are in fact, I think, expressing a belief in the system—framing it this way, the question becomes: can the system live up to that belief?

This is why in focusing upon Barack Obama, whatever one might think of him as a politician (and setting aside the irrationally partisan and race-driven attacks upon him and his family, there are critiques and dissatisfactions that a sober and reasonable person may have with his performance), it is worth looking at him as an individual. In my view, in many ways Obama is likely the most important Black man in history, beyond Martin Luther King, beyond Nelson Mandela. This is not because of his celebrity or his accomplishments while in office (or lack thereof), but rather because of the way he matter-of-factly mastered and rose through the tests and trials of American society. To put it simply, he won the highest political prize of our society, playing by the rules. He battled and prevailed in many different arenas: academia, law, publishing, politics. He learned the ways that things worked, how achievement is accomplished in the secular world, which was very important because so much previous outsize Black accomplishment had been based in the church. He showed a path.

Obama's life and career is a model for middle- and working-class Blacks and people of color of how to progress to the highest reaches of our society: work hard, get educated, get qualified, learn how to contest the career and workplace circumstances you find yourself in, and with a little timing, a little luck, who knows what might happen. *Endure.* Obama mastered the politics of Harvard Law School, the politics of Chicago, the politics of the Democratic Party, and the politics of national elections. And he did it "just like everybody else," learning the traditions and rules of each context. His was the next step in African American progress in society, following on Black athletes and business executives, an evolution in which he stated his case to the electorate and received their endorsement. One would think that right-wing whites, whether they agreed with his politics or not, whether they liked Black people or not, would see that career and achievement as something to be celebrated, something to be pointed at, not because of any "Kumbaya" racial fellow feeling, *but because it gave encouragement to the millions of young Blacks and other folks of color that they had a chance in this society—that the way for them to advance their hopes and dreams was in the library and at the ballot box, not in the streets.*

This, of course, was not apparently the lesson that everyone took from Obama's success. Large numbers of whites—a majority of whites?—interpreted the success of Barack Obama as a mortal threat to the future of the nation and after an eight-year drumbeat of opposition and rancor against him in reaction elected a successor who, on the face of all observable data, was uniquely unsuited and unqualified to be president, a man whose principal talent seemed (and seems) to lie in *not* discussing in any measurable detail any of the myriad issues and dangers facing our nation and society. It was enough to scream "Make America great again," which was a new or parallel iteration of the previous war chant to "Take our country back" and was surprisingly, shockingly effective at reviving the old racist spirits of the John Birch Society, the White Citizens' Councils, the KKK, and Father Charles Coughlin, among old lowlights of the right-wing past. Left unsaid in those reductive slogans was exactly how and why America was no longer a great country—a view that was seemingly contradicted by the concurrent, and ironic, claim that the nation had to be guarded from being overrun by the millions of illegal unworthies who were incessantly trying to sneak in and steal the MAGA birthright—and who the country had to be taken back *from*. Though the simultaneous advent of the chant by the Tea Party, which blossomed with the election of Obama, gave a serious hint as to who had illegitimately claimed it.

But I should stop there, as I do not wish here to go too far down the road of political mockery and snark. There are much more important things that I wish to discuss that go beyond the outcome of any one election, that go ultimately, I think, beyond politics, deeper than politics. They go to the figurative soul of the nation and can continue to be ignored or toyed with only at our deepest peril. And unfortunately, we have allowed these issues of national soul to become entangled in partisan politics. This entanglement is probably inevitable, and even articulating the issue in that frame may sound terribly naive, but wishful naivete does not diminish its truth.

The way that Obama was treated as president, whether through the obstinate opposition of Republican legislators or the disrespectful disdain of groups such as the birthers and the Tea Party, which have morphed into MAGA and Trumpism, is often excused as an exercise of tactics, a lawful utilization of the rules that is open to any partisan. But for me, there is a deep sadness in realizing just how much what might or could have been construed as sincere progress amid American complexity—gained after centuries of struggle and survival, and decades of applied strategy and hard work and following the rules, all of it paid for by the sacrifices, including the deaths, of millions—was seen as *defeat* by a significant number of whites. Obama's election was construed not as a healing or next step in the history of the nation but as a *wound*. And that that sense of wound was deliberately salted by, among others, Mitch McConnell, Rupert Murdoch, Paul Ryan, Roger Ailes, Tucker Carlson, and, yes, Donald Trump, is, to those who hope for a nation that can live up to its founding documents and provide sustaining shelter for all of its citizens, beyond tragic. And I'm pretty sure I'm not the only person, Black, white, Latino, Asian, or Native American, who feels that way.

I cannot help but feel that the tactics and the overall strategy—even if, perhaps *especially* if, they were merely political—have endangered our civil society. Not because those tactics prohibited Obama from achieving some of his political goals. The first bit of conclusive evidence toward this might lie in the events of another January morning, the sixth in 2021, and the ever-spreading malaise that is Trump's big lie regarding his loss to Joe Biden. But there are other dimensions that have been, I think, overlooked and that are to me a source of profound disappointment and confusion as to how large numbers of my purported fellow citizens see our past, present, and future. If we even define those words in the same ways. In my view, the message that was sent, deliberately, to Blacks and people of color throughout Obama's presidency and that culminated in Trump's campaign and continued on into and through his presidency was this: Even if you make it to Harvard Law, become a United States senator, win not one but two elections to become president, if you happen to be Black, *you are still illegitimate. You are not good enough. You are a usurper and a threat to all that is good and holy.*

Whether sincere belief or implementation of tactics, such statements do not enter into a vacuum. And it was different from the disparagement of Bill Clinton because it was based on race (also, Obama has been uniquely free of scandal). The way Obama was regarded and treated by large segments of the population tells other segments of the population that trying to live up to the rules and standards of the wider society doesn't really matter because, again, it won't be good enough. You, who on one day is vilified for not punishing bankers, will on the next be vilified as a socialist determined to undo capitalism. You will be accused of being a "Muslim," though you testify to Christian belief and have decades of publicized Christian practice behind you. Millions (including large percentages of the GOP) will state firmly that you are not a citizen. Your academic accomplishments will be questioned, undermined, and, in another strange twist, even mocked. Almost anything someone can think of to say, no matter how scurrilous or unlikely, about your mother, your wife, your children, you, will be posted to the Facebook newsfeed and passed around the country through the fiber-optic lines at the speed of light. And on and on and on. This is what you have to look forward to after gaining the skills and mustering the will necessary to win an election as president of the United States.

And it will be deliberately or ignorantly unnoted by a large segment of the populace that these are all very dangerous things to say and do, First Amendment or not (though they will cloak their abuse and irrationality in the robes of "free speech"). Because to note that would be to admit that such behavior begins to undermine the social contract and unravel the social fabric of our society. That contract, that fabric, they are fragile things to begin with, rightly celebrated as among the rarest of accomplishments in human history, in dire need of being handled with care and respect. Which, throughout the persecution of Barack Obama, and continuing into the campaigns and presidency of Donald Trump, they were not. Because people are watching, our children, including the white children at grammar schools who began to terrorize classmates of color with violence and chants of "Trump! Trump! Trump!," and people from other countries around the world who look to the United States for guidance, example, and salve.

As an African American, it is dispiriting to confirm private paranoias that large numbers of whites still prefer the old ways and are transferring those preferences to their children, or at the very least, they do not care *enough* about the way things appear to others to take those differences of interpretation and sensibility into account, or even value them as having weight. It becomes, I think, a subtle form of white supremacy, a way of saying that the desires and perceptions of whites take precedence over those of everyone else. It is a way of saying, quietly, that everyone else is subordinate. It is, in fact, a form of childishness, the sort of selfishness one expects from a toddler, writ large. And it is something that, in 2016, in 2020, in 2024, every day and every year on into the future, those others are not going to accept, so it will be a source of ongoing friction, and because of the volatile nature of the friction, it holds a danger of bursting into flame.

Perhaps some whites are unable to hear or perceive the provocation in the language of Donald Trump and many of his supporters. Think of Trump's reference to "the" African Americans, "the" Hispanics, "the" Muslims, and the way that article distances those described groups and implies that they are not part of a normal mainstream. Personally, I think Trump's supporters can hear that provocation, and they search for ways to excuse it. In any event, I believe all Americans should learn to hear it because it is so crucial to the ongoing daily life of the nation. Choosing the language and posturing of the Donald Trump of the 2016 presidential campaigns and as president, and later as a private citizen after leaving the White House, is a betrayal of the citizens who have paid taxes, served in the military, volunteered in our common civil society, and been law abiding coworkers, neighbors, relatives, and citizens. It is a deliberatively chosen ignorance in service of a nostalgia-fueled half dream of a time that never was, and can certainly never be.

Even in the best of times we underestimate just how thoroughly race is laced throughout our society—it is pervasive, in everything and found everywhere. Bringing this up can, I understand, make some whites uncomfortable. It is a painful and shameful legacy to be attached to, especially when one feels no personal real-time connection to the actions of the past. Also, such discussion can be construed as striving for power within an interaction or relationship, in the sense of trying to impose guilt or extract unearned advantage. In the best, and best-intentioned, of situations it can wrong-foot a conversation or situation, and thus it becomes in the interest of many whites, even those who consider themselves "woke," to use the current slang so egregiously abused by right-wingers, to encourage or even impose a zone of silence around all discussion of race—the same silence we see red state polities attempting to impose as a matter of law. And Blacks can also feel the awkwardness and choose avoidance or at times be either unintentionally clumsy or deliberately provocative in ways that become unproductive. As I have written elsewhere, it is almost as if we require "rules" for the discussion of race, which would have to be studied and acknowledged before one were allowed to participate in any discussions. (That, of course, presumes one would be willing to participate.)

But the zone of silence prevents us from intervening when race truly should be discussed. And when Obama left office, we found ourselves in one of those periods.

There are so many silences in American life and experience, so much unsaid, so many regrets—and there are those who feel absolutely nothing about the past and those, even, who glory in the cruelty and suffering. Then there are different layers of memory, different time zones of experience where people live in different zones of perception. How can we expect them to reconcile?

I have thought for some time that the next moment of progress in building our more perfect union was going to have to come from whites. In several different ways. Those whites who find themselves enamored of the MAGA and Trumpist dream are going to have to decide among themselves what kind of nation they want, whether they want to pursue a chimera of the past, and try to maintain a position of dominance that will trigger reaction and conflict, or whether they can imagine and work toward "liberty and justice for all." They have to decide whether they truly believe that "all men are created equal." Because those next steps of progress will involve things that only whites can do: stop fanning racial conflict, truly begin to try to bring an to end segregation, and see that every child in America has a real chance at an education that will equip him or her to compete in the new economy (many white children need this guarantee as well). It may be that class also enters the discussion here, but it is an open question as to whether there will ever be a time when class interest is more important to many white voters than a fantasy of white racial solidarity and dominance; I say fantasy because inequality grows by the day, and the "elite" pluto-crats that poor-, middle-, and working-class whites often support are laboring steadily to take such gains as have been made by average Americans during the past one hundred years. Yet white racial solidarity is as ferocious as it has been in decades, reignited by the presidency of Barack Obama and brought to a ferocious fury by the an-tics of Donald Trump.

After Obama, America stands revealed to itself, fac-ing the most painful, almost unbearable, self-knowledge, caught in a moment when lessons of the past are not going to be much help. It is time, finally, to imagine a sustainable future, as the past carries too much grievance, too much baggage, too much pain. Making America great again is in truth yet another relitigation of the '60s and '70s, of the '40s and '50s, of the '20s and '30s, of the 1840s, 1850s, 1860s, and, perhaps most specifically, of 1877. And as always, these relitigations, under whatever guise they are fought—class, taxes, social benefits, abortion, women's rights—are again entwined with the American third rail of race.

This revelation is a painful knowledge, in that we have much further to go than we thought, further than we may want to, or think we can, go. But the truth is, we are likely just beginning to enter into true accounting and discussion, at long last, as whites are being forced into the reckoning of American racial history and will have to decide if they want to go forward or go back (those who want to go back stand at the center of the red state desire to prevent the teaching of African American history).

But there is no staying the same.

I suspect that a vote for Donald Trump was and is not, as often stated, a vote to "shake things up," but rather a vote in pursuit of *not* changing, of *not* answering the challenges of the new America, both here now and coming, as well as of the world around the globe, with China rising, India fast on its heels, Russia wreaking havoc, Europe facing several kinds of change and unsettled civics, and Africa emerging into something no one can predict. And I have not even mentioned the looming challenges of climate change, unending Middle East conflict and the way it spills into the West, or the ultimately static economy that cannot seem to provide gains for all.

Trying to understand America in 2024 is like trying to solve an artificially intelligent Rubik's Cube, one programmed to outwit all attempts at solution and that continually reshuffles itself at great speed. Perhaps America can't be solved. Perhaps it can only be lived, and we only have a fifty-fifty chance of transcending political estrangement and polarization for the good of the future. Do enough of us see it as necessary to try? Or do too many of us want to reach backward for an allegedly better time?

For the first time in my adult life, I wonder if we can recapture the urgency and majority that sixty years ago led the nation to not just work but to *push* for a future that consciously broke with the mistakes of the past. I wonder if enough of us even want to. Or are there too many pressures and problems from too many different directions that exist in so many incompatible contexts that the fault lines overload, maybe by accident, without us intending or noticing it happening, making the bloody, strife-filled saga that one might have hoped was brought to a close by Barack Obama look in fact like a children's story?

Making Myths, Betraying Our Past

MY MOTHER USED to tell me that it was a grave sin, perhaps the gravest, to question the interior spiritual life of another human being; it was also a very serious matter to speak ill of the dead. So, when I first sat in my living room watching the PBS *American Experience* documentary biography *George Wallace: Settin' the Woods on Fire*, I found myself striving mightily to live up to those admonitions, and failing. I also found myself wondering why I was allowing the filth of Wallace's invective and racist posturing into my home—the historical clips are that scalding—even in the good cause of education. Because I couldn't help wondering how much of what I was watching was actually educational and how much of it was something more like exculpation, an almost literal whitewashing of history that tried to cast some of the most fraught moments of the second half of the American twentieth century into a superficially "moving" redemption narrative.

Settin' the Woods on Fire (the very title seems a bit glib to me, more appropriate to its original purpose as the title of a rollicking Hank Williams tune than the story of one of the most dangerous politicians in our history) is much like the other biographical documentaries of politicians on PBS, such as those on Eisenhower, on Nixon, on the Kennedys, on the Roosevelts, to name several splendid ones I've seen: trenchant, compelling, and mostly accurate. But *accuracy* isn't exactly the issue when dealing with George Wallace because I'm sure all the facts presented here have been scrupulously checked and vetted, as is the practice of the network.

My concern has more to do with what has been left out, left in the library stacks and far depths of the internet that will not be searched by the millions for whom this film will become the official version.

I'm wondering how viewers will learn the full story of the gruesome suffering of federal judge Frank Johnson and his family, which was wrought by Wallace's self-aggrandizing vilification and by literal attacks at the hands of Wallace's supporters (among other things, the home of Judge Johnson's mother was firebombed). Johnson had ruled several times in favor of civil rights, including in support of Rosa Parks and striking down the racist bus laws of Montgomery, ruling in favor of desegregating the bus depot in Birmingham, sanctioning the Ku Klux Klan for harassment of Freedom Riders, and allowing the Selma March to take place over Wallace's strident opposition. Johnson received death threats, had a cross burned in his yard, and was cast from local white society. In my view, Judge Johnson and his family were the true American heroes, and one wonders if there shouldn't be a film in the series about them.

Then there is the story of Wallace's third wife, Lisa Taylor Wallace, which is also glossed over to the point of being completely left out. They were married only a short time, and I do not wish to hint or imply lurking scandal; I merely wonder, as a concerned viewer and informed lay student of southern history, why the marriage is not mentioned at all. Wallace's other wives, Lurleen and Cornelia, are covered in some detail. If Mrs. Taylor Wallace refused to participate, shouldn't this have been noted? The omission leads the thoughtful viewer to ask what else may not be included, even when so much is included, so skillfully, in the liberal version of mythmaking, ironically sanitizing the story of such a racist conservative.

Also missing is a light sprinkling of the skeptical Black folks like me who don't care to make nice with Wallace. I do not wish to cast any aspersions on those Blacks in the film, including people like the legendary Black Alabama hero J. L. Chestnut, who have forgiven if not forgotten Wallace and his mean legacy. Even granted the time constraints of the medium (the film is in two parts, for a total of three hours, and is widely available on streaming platforms, including YouTube), a little less smug gloating by the likes of the white Wallace confidante Tom Turnipseed and a little more cross-examination of the talking heads and the historical subject would have helped me to more easily swallow the bitter pill of American witness that this necessary reexamination of the recent past demands. There are plenty of legitimate reasons to distrust Wallace, and, after all the violence and vicious insult, plenty of reasons to reject any too-easy reconciliation of southern whites and southern Blacks. The ongoing, never-ending battle over voting rights and congressional districts in Alabama is a further illustration of this. The state of Alabama, controlled by white conservatives, has, as of late 2023, been willing to defy even the right-wing Roberts Supreme Court, which ordered the state to redo the racial gerrymandering that had been put in place.

THE STORY OF GEORGE Corley Wallace Jr. is a good story: too good a story, in my view. Like all good stories it invites the imposition of predetermined narrative strictures— initiation, struggle, sacrifice, and redemption all poured into three acts that are designed to progress in a certain way and make us feel good—that also make more palatable to the viewer what was mostly just chaotic and opportunistic low life. Wallace wasn't on the Joseph Campbell hero's journey, with its supposition of an innocent young trueheart who compromises in order to achieve his dreams, making alliance with violence and evil, only to learn and then correct the error. This is not a Hollywood movie we're watching; it's a documentary. I grow suspicious of the subtle ways in which I think this film is trying to move me with its definitively designed arc toward the emotionally rewarding third act, toward viewing Wallace as yet another American character who, like Henry Ford, like Douglas MacArthur, like Michael Jordan, went through his ups and downs, behaved egregiously at times and then suffered for it, and who, in so doing, earned the kind of burnished glow that we all recognize as the true historic countenance of every exalted figure Americans have loved since George Washington and Daniel Boone.

Another factor in this sort of storytelling that raises suspicions, and that is certainly a factor here, is the reflexive great-man meme of Western history (elaborated quite acutely by Ralph Waldo Emerson in *Representative Men*) and the peculiarly American love of the Saul-to-Paul "Road to Damascus" conversion narrative with its tropes of anagnorisis (that moment when the character makes a critical discovery) and penitential suffering and redemption. Why, aside from Americans' Christianity, is this ready-made story so appealing to us? Does it indulge our own sense of mischief and wrongdoing and suggest that all will be well— our souls laundered and folded—if we are contrite at the end of our lives? If we seek public pardon? This is part and parcel of American rhetoric and the emotive "testifying" and spectacle we expect from our public figures. So George Wallace, as his story is told in this documentary, fits right in; it also makes one wonder what the last few pages of Donald Trump's story might look like.

Another question: why do we in our society always try to package history—decades and decades of history, in this case, and the fates of millions of Americans—into the lives of single individuals? There is a tendency, I think, in this kind of mythmaking to revise reprobates into rogues, rogues into rascals, and rascals into beloved aunts and uncles. As when we see George Wallace, a man who consciously chose to ride the tiger of race through the vicious undercurrents of Alabama politics and American history at perhaps the worst possible moment, subject to a hagiography. Wallace skillfully, gleefully, fanned the fires of racial and cultural war—it would not be too much to say he fanned the flames of national heartache—in the 1960s. He is gradually turned by the film (not just by the film but also by time, the worst of all enemies of remembrance) into a kind of shambling, just-folks folk hero, and we are encouraged to forget the cold-blooded "outn----ring," in Wallace's infamous term, and gay-baiting of political opponents. We are supposed to overlook his telling of supporters to "remember you're white," his standing in the schoolhouse door, the police riot at Selma, the crisscrossing of the country year after year spewing racial invective high and low while inventing the "code words" later put so well to use by Nixon and Reagan and a host of lesser lights. If we allow all that to be forgotten, we betray our history, we betray what progress there is that has been purchased at so high a cost, and we betray our best selves.

In our embrace of the redemption myth, we have forgotten that it was George Wallace who so skillfully used "busing" to build his national base, venturing into the northern cities and convincing working-class whites in Boston, New York, Baltimore, and Chicago—to name four—that their interest lay in oppressing Blacks just as these workers had been oppressed by the robber barons and union haters. Might, for one example, the city of Boston been spared decades of trauma had Wallace not been so present in the national consciousness as an opponent of desegregation and especially busing?

In *Settin' the Woods on Fire*, we see Wallace gleefully describing how he is going to force President Nixon to abandon federal busing mandates and then take the credit among whites for the accomplishment. And so he does, and the rest is history—if we remember. Nixon, as was often his wont, performed a bit of presidential sleight of hand, expressing first his opposition to busing and his strong preference for the "neighborhood school" but then pivoting and saying that as president, he was subject to doing whatever the courts ordered. It might have been George Wallace's highest moment, having forced the hand of a president, which he had never before been able to do.

But, aside from Wallace "settin' the cities on fire," why was busing such a flash point to begin with? Why was it an existential danger back then in Boston and Milwaukee and so on as Wallace asserted? Why was it such a danger later on in, say, Hartford in the '90s and '00s? Why are "neighborhood schools" so vehemently defended to this day in places like New York City, when on the other hand, students will commute heroic distances to attend selective or magnet schools that will help them realize their goals? I live in a rural state, Maine, in which the majority of our schoolchildren utilize the yellow behemoths as their only transportation daily; busing itself could not be any more routine or banal an activity, yet even today the word still carries the divisive and negatively emotional currents Wallace gave it. The issue was not, in fact, "busing"; the issue was "*desegregation* busing," or bringing white children in proximity to black children.

Busing was always going to be a tough sell to Americans, Black or white (Black parents were not crazy about sending their children into unwelcoming places that often became quasi-combat zones), but it was and is exacerbated because George Wallace used the issue to deliberately

divide American from American in their native land, simply to chase the mess of pottage, some might say, that is the
presidency. *He was willing to destroy the social fabric of the nation in order to advance his private goals.* And though he wasn't
very good or successful at chasing the presidency, he was
quite good and incredibly successful at dividing us. I am not
being revisionist. We live out the results and implications of
the intentional actions of George Corley Wallace Jr. every
single day in this country, in the battles over voting rights
and federal appropriations, in the polarized struggle over
federal resources and historical truth. The virus of race,
cultured and carefully misted by George Wallace, has in-
fected every corner and precinct of the nation.

The sins, if I may use so charged a word, of George
Wallace, the social conservative and big-government hater
(who, as far as I can tell, never, once he left college, cashed
a nongovernmental payroll check), are manifold, too manifold to enumerate. I could have pity for the man I would see
on my television screen suffering so grievously in his wheel-
chair because of an assassination attempt—or perhaps
forgiveness is, as my mother would say, between him and
his God. But I have come to see George Wallace as a sort
of Promethean figure in American cultural history—let's
not reduce him just to politics—and when he stole the firebrand of race, he set off a blaze that couldn't be put out. He
set aflame a conflagration that chases us to this day, burning through our hearts and through our cities and towns,
infecting our policing and our real estate and banking sec-
tors, our healthcare system and our environment. And yes,
it might have happened anyway, and yes, it might have
been someone else—Jesse Helms or Strom Thurmond, to

name two masters during that time in American history of "outn----ring"—but it was him, and it was what he wanted. He chose it.

Who knows? Maybe that church in Birmingham would have been bombed anyway; maybe those four girls would have died anyway. Maybe Viola Liuzzo was meant to be killed in a drive-by shooting on a lonely Alabama country road. Maybe Jimmie Lee Jackson was supposed to be gutshot and die in front of his mother. Maybe Ted Landsmark would have been stabbed and beaten with an American flag and huge flagpole while walking past an antibusing protest in Boston anyway. But when you think about those supremacists and nationalists marching through Charlottesville carrying tiki torches yelling about being "replaced," and when you think about Heather Heyer, the woman who was struck and killed the next day, think about George Wallace, standing in the schoolhouse door, egging the haters on.

Wallace is far from the only American politician to receive this sort of redemptive second chance that allows questionable behavior to be forgiven and reworked into redemptive myth, or even forgotten. The two most prominent on the national stage might be Richard Nixon, who evolved into a kind of national sage and advisor emeritus after the national trauma of Watergate, and Edward Kennedy, who became a beloved folk hero and liberal standard-bearer after his dishonorable actions surrounding the accident at Chappaquiddick and the resulting death of Mary Jo Kopechne; Kennedy had also been dismissed from Harvard for cheating as an undergraduate and was admitted to law school at the University of Virginia, even though that broke long-established rules at the school about what kind of past academic and personal behavior would and would not be tolerated.

And when thinking about redemptive mythmaking, we cannot forget another legendary southern politician, Bill Clinton, who survived a constellation of scandal over time that would have doomed almost anyone else. Clinton illustrates the trick: Admit you've sinned, ask for forgiveness, promise to do better. Weaponize Christianity by illustrating that you have given all your digressions serious thought and that you know you're wrong. However subtle or overt the individualized process, the public is allowed (supposed) to participate in the catharsis. President "It depends on what the meaning of 'is' is" was perhaps the best in history at this prestidigitation.

Back to George Wallace. Maybe his apology was sincere; maybe all his conjecture about "Saint Paul on the road to Damascus" was the result of years of "trying to remove the thorn," suffering as Saint Paul did after his amazing conversion from persecutor of Christians to Jesus's most devoted apostle. But it can also be seen as a masterly appropriation of one of the most potent Christian stories by a master politician, who only asked for Blacks—those most Christian and evangelical of all Americans, who also always love a good redemption story—to forgive him when he needed them in the '70s and '80s (after voting rights) to help him win elections. Only God knows, and only God, not liberals, not PBS, not the film's "downtrodden, suffering Blacks of Alabama," not Congressman John Lewis, and especially not me can forgive him. May God and my mother forgive me.

⌘

LET'S NOT GET CARRIED away here. George Wallace, already
faded into what feels like so far in the past, did not invent
racism in America, past or present. He was merely a skilled
opportunist who, like many before and since, took advantage of what he saw as an opening in a career as a professional politician. *Settin' the Woods on Fire* does do a service in
illuminating the human side of Wallace. One man cannot
create that much evil by himself, not even George Wallace,
the George Wallace who started out wanting to emulate
FDR, who was considered the fairest white judge in his part
of Alabama, and who sold his ideals for the devil of race,
while egging on every societal regressive impulse at a time of
national crisis. Wallace chose to be a transformer—in the
electrical engineering meaning of the term, transferring energy from one circuit to multiple circuits—of *racial* energy
and emotion in American history and civilization. He
paid for his audacity, big mouth, and that cocky strut into
infamy. He paid.

But millions of Americans voted for him, and millions
more voted for his political descendants: Richard Nixon,
Ronald Reagan, Pat Buchanan, George H. "Willie Horton"
Bush, and, yes, Rudy Giuliani, and Mitch McConnell, and
Marjorie Taylor Greene, and Paul Gosar, and Matt Gaetz,
and Ron DeSantis, and Donald Trump. And, to name a
Democrat, the aforementioned William Jefferson Clinton,
who we should not forget allowed the execution of a brain
damaged and helpless Ricky Rector in the early days of
his first presidential campaign to ensure that he, the liberal, didn't get outn----red either. (He also deliberately hu-
miliated a young Black woman, the rapper Sister Souljah,
who had spoken foolishly but did not deserve to have the

national spotlight directed at her in order to prove a politician's "not-scared-of-Blacks" bona fides.) That's what scares me the most about *George Wallace: Settin' the Woods on Fire* and other films and books like it: one man didn't do all that, couldn't have, and it seems that all the rest, the millions upon millions who vote for and cheer on such men, are getting off easy.

Speech at Ole Miss

A keynote given August 14, 1999, to the first-year students entering the honors college at the University of Mississippi.

FORTY YEARS AGO, longer than I have lived, and more than twice as long as most of you have lived, the thought of a person such as myself standing here at a podium talking to the honor students entering the University of Mississippi would not only have been ludicrous, it would have been unthinkable.

Now those of you who are young—and you are very young, though I'm sure you are quite determined to think yourselves otherwise—probably find it hard to accept the Mississippi of forty, fifty, one hundred years ago as a place that actually existed. It probably doesn't mean much to you now, and we'll get to that in a moment. But let us pause for a second to reflect on the fact that I am standing here, thirty-seven years to the semester after the integration of the University of Mississippi. That process, integrating the University of Mississippi, was one of the symbolic—not to mention literal—battlegrounds in the struggle for racial equality in the United States; the University of Mississippi is the place that some would say is the site of the last unofficial battle of the Civil War, and a place where others would say that war is still being fought. The fact that I am here today says something about America. I think what it says is good. It is a story of the malleability of American society and the American system, of our ability to adjust to and absorb change. This malleability is not something to be taken for granted, as can be witnessed through the tragedies that have occurred in this decade in Bosnia, in Rwanda, and in Kosovo. Oftentimes these complex, multifaceted conflicts extend in some part from the inability to, shall we say, *manage* history.

What I mean by that vaguely menacing phrase is that the legacy of a historical past, which we can loosely call "context," bumps into the pressures and processes of change. The developing momentum of present and future is held back, *dragged* back, by the weight of the past. The events of the present take place, in effect, *in* the past, in the atmosphere and climate that is created by what has gone before. It is this intersection of past and present that I find so intriguing, and that is what led to my writing the book *Mississippi*. This is also what makes our presence here today noteworthy. All of us here represent the possibility of, and openness to, change that exists in America, as well as the intersection of past and present that subtly and not-so-subtly governs our existence. Or you can think of it another way, in the words of Mississippi's Nobel laureate, William Faulkner: "The past is never dead. It's not even past."

THE SUBTITLE OF MY book *Mississippi* is *An American Journey*. At the risk of sounding hackneyed, it's a story that could have happened only in America—one unique to the American phenomenon of brutal human nature, how we act when there is property and money to be gained, contradicted by the rule of law, namely the Constitution, which fiercely proclaims the right of humans, *all* humans, to be left to their own devices while also being treated with equity and justice.

Henry James, one of the most subtle analysts of the human condition ever to put pen to paper, wrote: "It's a complex fate, being an American." We usually think there is something akin to winning the lottery in being lucky enough to be an American, given the other sorts of fates that await many citizens in other parts of the world. James made me contemplate whether there is something unique, something inherently different, about being citizens of the United States that distinguishes us from the citizens of France, China, or Brazil. If so, what might it be? How might it be? How might it apply to me?

These are the sorts of questions I was being forced to confront both by events in my own life—experiences of blatant racism in New York—and national events that occurred in the months and years before I began writing *Mississippi*. The racial baiting and insensitivity of the Reagan years, which I think reintroduced a level of meanness to heretofore gradually improving racial matters, the use and misuse of Willie Horton in the 1988 presidential campaign, the ever-widening gulf in perception between Blacks and whites on racial subjects—all these and more—contributed to a profound personal malaise. First of all, of course, there was my own life, the life I lived in my family and community growing up in suburban Chicago, a life that gave me a certain set of experiences and expectations. I led a privileged childhood and adolescence, but I found the world getting ever more difficult and constricting, racially and culturally speaking, as I got older.

Through an extensive encounter with the book *From Behind the Veil* by Yale professor Robert Stepto, I had been thinking about autobiographical texts as they specifically related to African Americans. In his book, Professor Stepto outlined a tradition of Black American autobiography dating from slave narratives—books like Frederick Douglass's *Narrative* and Booker T. Washington's *Up from Slavery*—and illuminated the central role these texts have played in African American letters. I had been intrigued by this tradition for a number of years and had wondered what kind of new book might explore it—live up to it—but extend it to the present.

At the same time, because of Susan Sontag's class on the history of the autobiography that I had taken in graduate school at Brown University, I was interested by the idea of the memoir as a Western practice dating from Saint Augustine and Michel de Montaigne. I got into the habit of reading autobiographies and nonfiction books written in the first person. I became particularly enamored of two masterpieces: *The Songlines* by Bruce Chatwin and *Labyrinth of Solitude* by Octavio Paz. I was so awed by these two texts, and still am, that I wanted to write something like them, in emulation or homage. I mention this because those of you who want to be writers have to be aware that books are made out of other books, and writers are made from readers.

What I learned from those two books, *The Songlines* and *Labyrinth of Solitude*, was how deeply a writer could go into him or herself, beyond the standard "I was born at 22 Maple Street in Sewickley, Pennsylvania, etc., etc." They showed me how the self had to do with *context* in all of its manifestations. We live under the aegis of gender, nation, race, geography, history, family, religion, class—the list goes on and on—and in deciphering myself, I wanted to take into account as many of these contexts as I could.

So I set off on what would become a four-year odyssey through the counties and libraries of Mississippi, trying to discover the place my parents had come from, in the hope that it would tell me something about myself. I drove up and down and across the state from the summer of 1990 through the spring of 1994, sometimes with family members, sometimes with friends, most often by myself. I would read up on an area or aspect of the state, then I would try to explore it and get a feel for it. In this I was aided by the generosity of many Mississippians, Black and white, who would steer me to a person or a place and often call ahead to make sure I was well received. One person in particular who helped me was my friend Kristina Ford. She seemed not only to know, personally, most of the women in the state, but she also carried such authority with them that they would trust me and graciously accede to whatever imposition I requested, be it an interview, a guided tour, or a place to crash. In this way I learned a side of Mississippi, the human side, that I might otherwise have missed, and it greatly complicated my vision of the state and, I hope, saved me from any number of easy misconceptions.

One such episode involved Mrs. Celeste Luckett of Clarksdale, an elderly white woman of substantial means with a home so grand I felt as if I were stepping into *Gone with the Wind* or *Cat on a Hot Tin Roof*. I had never talked to anyone like her, and she had never talked to anyone like me—meaning, she told me, an educated Black man who assumed equality. We were both extremely wary as we sat down to tea in her family room. But in a turn that was an education for me in the humanity of others, that is, don't assume you know who you are talking to, she asked me what I thought of *The Silence of the Lambs*. (Thomas Harris, "the only other writer [she'd] ever met," was the son of a close friend.) When I said, "I think *Red Dragon* is a much better book," she smiled broadly, and we launched into a long and detailed talk about mystery writers that set the tone for the warm and open conversation that I draw from in *Mississippi*.

And I had this sort of experience time and again. I went on a tour of antebellum mansions in Natchez with deep trepidation and found my presence almost, apparently, unnoticed. I spent weeks at a time here in Oxford without experiencing any of what my fertile imagination had steeled me against. I drove through what were for me the scariest parts of the state, the southwestern corridor from, say, Woodville—legendary for its ferocious opposition to the Civil Rights Movement—through Amite County, over to Poplarville, site of the lynching of Mack Charles Parker, without incident. I went into small-town libraries and was given the help I requested. I discovered Mississippi as a living, breathing place, as complex as any other, and I was able to develop and modify my thinking, and, more importantly, to stop seeing the state in a demonized fashion. It no longer made me nervous merely to hear the word *Mississippi*; I could look at it as a place in America, with all that meant, for better and for worse.

But not just *any* place. I still had to recognize and reckon with everything that happened here. It was quite disconcerting for me to learn, as an American, as a young person, and as a Black man, some of the events that had occurred here, and that knowledge has shadowed my life and imagination to this day. I expect it always will. But that's why I think we have to explore our true history, why we have to dive into context—so that we can, if not master it, at least come to understand it in a way that keeps it from mastering us. In America, the actual battles of the past never truly disappear but instead go underground and become symbolic battles. We don't need the US Army at Ole Miss or fire hoses in Birmingham to fight out our beliefs on racial equality; now we squabble endlessly over affirmative action, welfare, and the criminal justice system.

What I have learned from my long affair with Mississippi is that American's greatest strength, and its greatest weakness, is our belief in second chances, our belief that we can always start over, that things can be made better, transcended, erased. This is weakness when it leads us to seek easy forgiveness and easy solutions, when we declare that history is over, when we deny the pain of the past and the present in our desperate desire to believe that we are moving forward. Because positive change, like most good things, is deceptive. We often think we're doing better than we are, and sometimes we're merely relieved to stop and catch our breath when we really need to be pushing on.

Our hope and ability to change is a strength when we channel this impetus to examine ourselves honestly—who we are, where we have come from, and the context that has shaped us and that we in turn have to shape. When we recognize that it is only by embracing our individual and collective weaknesses that we can truly begin to choose our future. These are the things I learned from studying Mississippi, the state, and writing *Mississippi*, the book. I like to think that I began to free myself, or at least got a long way down the road in that direction. I say *began* to free myself because I don't think I'm there yet. I don't think America is. I don't think we can be. There is too much left to do. Are we free? Are you free? Are any of you sitting here, Black or white, truly free of all that's happened, of our collective past? That is what you must ask your-selves, and then think about your obligation as a student at the University of Mississippi, as a citizen of the state of Mississippi, and as a citizen of the United States. How do we free ourselves from a past that none of us created and that few of us wish to maintain?

It has become fashionable at this time in the nation's history to decry the hopelessness of Gunnar Myrdal's American Dilemma: the inability of Americans to live up to our stated creeds and promises, particularly on the issue of race. I am perhaps as guilty of this behavior as anyone, but when I began to think of a few words to say to you all, Mississippi's best and brightest, I kept coming back to the theme of hope, something that even in his darkest hours in Memphis on the night of April 3, 1968—the night before he died—Dr. Martin Luther King never lost. That night, harried, weary, depressed, under constant death threats, and—who knows—possibly with a premonition of his assassination, he said, "Only when it is dark can we see the stars." He went on to talk about what the Movement had accomplished, what was left to be done, how he was certain his goals would, one day, be realized. I have yet to understand how a man under such pressure could still believe, and I probably never will.

But it got me thinking about a trip I took to Atlanta a few years ago. I was met at the airport by a business associate, a white woman about fifty years old. While we were riding into the city in her spanking new BMW, she asked me if I had ever seen Martin Luther King Jr.'s tomb. I hadn't, and we had a few minutes, so she drove to the Atlanta ward of Dr. King's youth, Sweet Auburn. As we walked through the Black neighborhood where the tomb is located, I realized that my friend, Mary, was speaking about ninety miles an hour in her molasses drawl and saying, *Dr.-King-said-this-and-Dr.-King-said-that-and-do-you-remember-when-Dr.-King-went-there-and-what-he-did* . . . And I thought, what is going on here, all this talk of Dr. King? Then it occurred to me that he belonged to Mary, a blond white woman from Macon, Georgia, driving her fancy car, just as much as he belonged to me. She had, in fact, heard him better than a lot of Black folks I know.

Something else I thought about, as we stood by the reflecting pool surrounding the tomb, was another portion of the sermon Dr. King gave that night before he was killed: "I just want to do God's will, and He's allowed me to go up to the mountain . . . And I've seen the Promised Land. I may not get there with you. But I want you to know tonight, that we, as a people, will get to the Promised Land . . . Mine eyes have seen the glory of the coming of the Lord."

In this metaphor, Dr. King, who had seen firsthand all the hate and death, the jail and water hoses and burning churches of the Civil Rights Movement, was describing himself as a sort of Moses, the prophet of the Israelites who didn't make it to the Promised Land, either. Most of the things Dr. King said have turned out to be true, and the implications of what he said the night before he died are, for those of us who remain, chilling, and a tremendous challenge. It comes down to leadership, and this is what I would like to say to the young people here this afternoon: If Dr. King was our American Moses, the one who showed us that we could imagine a way toward the reconciliation of the present and the past, that we could find a path out of the collective enslavement with which our tragic history binds and blinds us, where are the Joshuas, Deborahs, Gideons, and Samuels willing to lead the rest of the way? I would submit that they are sitting in those chairs out there in this auditorium, that when you stand up to walk out, you will be looking at them, and as you leave here for the vital endeavor of your education, if there is only one thing you retain from all I have said today, that is the one thing I would like for you to remember.

Technology vs. African Americans

1.

I N THE MID-'90S, still relatively early in the era of personal computing, a friend of mine in New York City owned a one-man computer firm specializing in the design and construction of internet websites. This was when there was something still magical and unique about the commercial, entertainment, and informational junctions in cyberspace that could be visited from individual computers around the world. I put it that way just to emphasize that websites, even the World Wide Web itself, were not invented until 1989 and did not appear until 1990. So when my friend started building these sites on the internet (which few of us then even knew existed), it seemed like an act of magic, if not alchemy.

What was astonishing to me was that from time to time he would contract for more work than he could handle, and then he would post an electronic want ad, usually on an internet message board, stating the number of lines of computer code to be written, the requisite computer language, the specific functions of the program being built, and the pay he was offering per line.

That ad would often be answered by programmers from, as might be expected, Silicon Valley towns like San Jose and Palo Alto, or from Austin, Texas, or Cambridge, Massachusetts. Which seemed miraculous in and of itself. The respondent might be someone recently laid off from Digital, a hacking grad student at MIT, or a precocious thirteen-year-old who had learned the C++ language as an extra-credit project in middle school. The work was sent out over the internet and sent back ready to be incorporated into my friend's project as a building block of a much larger system. These programmers, whoever they were and wherever they were from, proved reliable and punctual; their transactions, miraculous to the uninitiated, were so commonplace in the digital kingdom as to go unremarked.

Shortly after my friend began hiring extra help to grow his capability, he started getting responses from programmers in India. The Indians, often from the subcontinent's technological center of Bangalore, were skilled, literate, and, best of all, both fast and very cheap—a contractor's dream. Accordingly, he parceled out more and more programming to them and less and less to Americans. Not so patriotic, but isn't that what GATT and NAFTA and all the other free trade treaties are all about?

Stories like that are usually presented as cautionary tales about the loss of American jobs to the hungry masses of the developing world. But there was another troubling aspect to this story, one that loomed larger for me as I learned about what my friend did in his business and *how* he did it. That troubling aspect remains, twenty-five years later: Why weren't more African Americans involved in these developments, this generational if not epochal business revolution? The activity was so clean, so sophisticated, and so lucrative; not least of all, it felt like the future. And it didn't take connections or a long apprenticeship to jump in. Just savvy and know-how.

I first began thinking about these issues more seriously after viewing the computer journalist Robert X. Cringely's 1996 documentary film *Triumph of the Nerds*, about the creation of the Bill Gates and Steve Jobs generation of the cyberelite. Cringely had spent time with young people at swap meets, watching them become entranced with electronics and the technological future, building their own machines and dreaming of starting the next Apple. There were no Blacks in sight. Young Black Americans, who could have been cashing in on the bonanza that was then buzzing through cyberspace, *didn't appear to be aware of it.* What kind of job could have been more appropriate for a technologically literate inner-city youth than to perform this kind of service? Conceivably, it could be done. No apprenticeship or connections were needed, and the field didn't require any capital outlay: one could, theoretically, surf the net at school or the public library, get the assignment and specs, and send the finished code back to whomever had commissioned it. And get paid. Democratic guerrilla capitalism. "Good jobs at good wages," as former Massachusetts governor Michael Dukakis, the 1988 presidential hopeful (undone by, among other things, the Willie Horton ad), was fond of saying.

There were high school kids working part time utilizing high-tech skills and college kids who were dropping out of school to work in the computer industry, if not starting their own companies. And as for the kids at Cringely's swap meet, it's not *likely* that any of them would start the next big thing, but it was at least possible. Jobs and Gates had done it. Apple, Hewlett-Packard, and Oracle, just to mention three of the most successful and highly capitalized companies in the history of American business, with a combined stock market value well into the trillions, were all started with almost no capital by folks fooling around in their garages. Later on, companies like Google, Facebook, and Amazon would follow the same path.

In the mid-'90s I found myself wondering where were the armies of ghetto youths ready to meet the innovation and programming needs of an exponentially expanding electronic frontier and get rich in the process, in what was perhaps the last gold rush in American history? I am, decades later, still wondering.

2.

THE HISTORY OF AFRICAN Americans during the past four hundred years is traditionally narrated as an ongoing struggle against oppression and indifference on the part of the American mainstream, a struggle charted as an upward arc progressing toward ever more justice and opportunity. This description is not without accuracy, but there is another, equally true way of narrating that history, and its implications are as frightening for the nation as a whole as they are for Blacks as a group: the history of African Americans since the discovery of the New World is the story of their encounter with technology, an encounter that has proved perhaps irremediably devastating to their hopes, dreams, and possibilities.

From the caravels, compasses, navigational techniques, and firearms of the first Portuguese explorers who reached the coast of West Africa in the 1440s to the never-ending Moore's Law expansion of microchip computing power and its ongoing social, military, and media implications for our society, the Black community has had one negative encounter after another with the technological innovations of the mainstream. Within American history this aspect of Blacks' experience is unique. One might argue that the disadvantageous situation of Blacks vis-à-vis technology has as much to do with issues of class and wealth as it does with race, but such a critique verges on, I think, the disingenuous. As a group, Blacks still lag well behind whites economically (with all the implications and outcomes implied and inherent in those deficits), and they have often suffered from the uses of technology in ways that other groups have not. In fact, they were often intentionally singled out to suffer. Poor whites, non-Black Hispanics, and Asians were not dragged from their native lands to work as slaves and then buffeted for hundreds of years by the vagaries of technology and an economy and legal regime they did not understand, much less control. The historical experience of each ethnic group in the history of the United States is unique and composed of its own problems and opportunities (or lack thereof), but none of them are comparable to that of African Americans, a circumstance that remains true until this day.

What is intriguing and deeply disturbing is that Blacks have participated as equals in the technological world only as consumers (principally, of cell phones and to a lesser extent social media and search engines), otherwise existing on the margins of the ethos that defines the nation, underrepresented as engineers, designers, innovators, and implementers of our systems and machines. As a group, they have I think suffered from something that can loosely be called technological illiteracy. Though this has not been the point of technological innovation, it has undeniably been its fallout. It has been important for a number of decades that our society understand and come to terms with this; having failed, it is difficult to understate the urgency that now exists given the societal and global difficulties—climate change, political strife, various demographic changes—that are developing, and there are technological developments in the making that could permanently affect the destiny of Black Americans, as Americans and as global citizens. Facial recognition, artificial intelligence, robotic automation, data mining, and genetically modified food are all made imperial by the algorithm, and all loom as existential threats. I also think it is safe to say that algorithms are not neutral, that carry within and with them the biases, intentional and unintentional, of their creators, and so if the algorithms that rule our society are the creations of white males they are going to carry the biases, intentional and unintentional, of those creators.

Is it so far-fetched to imagine a *Blade Runner*–like scenario in which Black ghettos such as South Central, West Baltimore, and Chicago's Wild 100s are sealed off and patrolled by drones utilizing facial recognition? The dark and frightening possibilities presented by the end of highly paid low-skilled labor, ever more powerful software and information machines, and the unresting and remorseless rapaciousness of global neoliberal capitalism renders traditional American policy disagreements over welfare, affirmative action, integration versus separatism, and the like trivial by comparison.

These issues go to the very marrow of Black experience in North America. They may also become a matter of survival for Blacks as a group and for the nation as a whole since those two fates are again and always inextricably connected. As the world gets faster and more information-centered, it also gets meaner: disparities of wealth and power strengthen; opportunities change and often fade away. How can Black Americans achieve the promise of America when that promise is largely, and increasingly, predicated on the sector of the country's economy (and history) that has proved most costly to them—when the disturbing outcome of their almost five hundred years of encountering Western technology and its practitioners is that many regard them as at best the stepchild of the American experiment?

3.

EUROPEANS HAD PROWLED THE Mediterranean for two thousand years, sailing from Greece to Rome, from Rome to Egypt, from Spain to Morocco, and on hundreds of other routes, before any systematic sailing craft or technique was developed. In the 1400s the Portuguese prince who came to be known as Henry the Navigator (1394–1460) dispatched a series of voyages to make maps and chart data; by the mid-1440s the Portuguese, in search of new, unexploited trade routes, had reached Cape Verde and the Senegal River.

As they worked their way down the northwestern African coast, the Portuguese came up against what seemed at first an insurmountable problem: strong winds and currents from the north meant that a ship returning to Lisbon would have to travel long distances against the wind. Enter the caravel, with its three masts and large sails—a perfectly designed solution to the problem and the machine that allowed Portugal to rule the waves from West Africa to India for a hundred years, much as the US Navy rules the waves today, and the American economy therefore rules the world.

The Atlantic slave trade was one of the industries that emerged from this new Portuguese capability. Western technology was involved with the rise of Black slavery in other ways as well: Arab and African slave traders exchanged their human chattels for textiles, metals, and firearms, all products of Western technological wizardry, and those same slavers used guns, vastly superior to African weapons of the time, in wars of conquest against those tribes whose members they wished to capture.

The slave wars and trade were only the first of many encounters with Western technology to prove disastrous for people of African descent. In the United States, as in South America and the Caribbean, the slaves were themselves the technology that allowed Europeans to master the wilderness. Then, in 1793, as the efficiency of the slave economy on cotton plantations (where slaves cost more to maintain than they could generate in profits) was being questioned in some quarters, Eli Whitney of Connecticut invented a simple gin that allowed harvested cotton to be picked clean of seeds—an essential step before milling—on a far greater scale than had previously been possible or imagined.

Suddenly rendered cost-efficient, cotton farming became a way to get rich quick. Thousands of Black Africans were imported to do the work; in Mississippi alone the number of slaves increased from 498 in 1784 to 195,211 by 1840. Here were the roots of the millions of African Americans who would come to populate the industrial Midwest, from Kansas City to Chicago to Pittsburgh to Buffalo. Those Blacks, in the great migrations following the world wars, would compose the urban proletariat that is both pouring forth Black success stories and struggling with social pathologies so difficult as to seem unsolvable.

The largest northward migration of Blacks took place during and after the Second World War. This exodus was largely a result of the invention of the mechanical cotton picker, another technological masterpiece that enabled three or four workers to perform a task that on some farms had required hundreds if not thousands of hands. Displaced by machinery and no longer needed in the underdeveloped American South, where they had been brought solely to do this kind of work, millions of Blacks went north to the industrial cities, where they encountered another kind of technology: the great factories of mass production. It was a violent shift for many whose families had known only agriculture for two hundred years. And the millions of Irish, Slavic, German, and Italian immigrants who were already there in those cities felt they'd done their time and were ready to move up; they resented the new competition that often drove down wages and exacerbated social tension and conflict that already existed. Many of the most vicious and enduring stereotypes about Blacks were born of this resentment.

When, less than fifty years later, those northern factories began closing and moving offshore, owing to the technologically advancing information and communications revolutions of the '70s, '80s, and '90s, Blacks were left behind in the inner cities of the Rustbelt, suffering from the metamorphosis of our society into a series of suburban megalopolises. Improvements in communications and transportation have struck the further blow of rendering the city irrelevant as a business and economic center, allowing mainstream money to be pulled out; the COVID-19 pandemic only further magnified and accelerated these trends as workers chose to stay at home and work remotely. The resulting isolation and deprivation, most eloquently outlined in the theories of the Harvard sociologist William Julius Wilson, account for the desolate urban landscapes we now see in parts of Detroit, Chicago, and Gary, Indiana, among many other Rustbelt and Southern cities.

Technology in and of itself is not at fault; it's much too simple to say that gunpowder or agricultural machinery or fiber optics has been the enemy of an entire group of people. A certain machine is put to work in a certain way—the purpose for which it was designed. The people who design the machines are not intent on unleashing chaos; they are usually trying to accomplish a task more quickly, cleanly, or cheaply, following the imperative of innovation and efficiency that has ruled Western civiliza-

tion since the Renaissance. But the *outcomes* of those innovations are unpredictable and often unmanageable, and
this is what we have seen again and again in our society
and civilization.

Yet another aspect of technology's great cost to Blacks
should be considered: while the Gilded Age roared through
the last part of the nineteenth century and Carnegie, Rockefeller, Vanderbilt, and others made the first great American
fortunes as they wired, tracked, and fueled the new industrial society, Blacks were mired in Reconstruction and its
successor, Jim Crow. This circumscription limited their life
prospects and, worse, those of their descendants. As the
great American technopolis was built, with its avatars from
Thomas Edison to Alfred P. Sloan to Bill Gates, Blacks were
locked out, politically, financially, and socially—and they
have found it difficult to work their way in. It is impossible
to calculate, for instance, the cost to African Americans
of them being locked out of the banking system for generations and being unable to accumulate wealth in the most
common and traditional way that white American families have done so: real estate. Instead, forced to rent and in
effect subsidize others, Black earnings and rent payments
have until very recently largely gone to create capital and
wealth for their oppressors and contribute to disparities
that we see before us.

4.

BLACKS HAVE TRADITIONALLY BEEN poorly educated—look
at the never-ending crises in urban public schools—and

deprived of the sorts of opportunities that create the vision necessary for technological ambition. Black folkways in America, those unspoken, largely unconscious patterns of thought and belief about what is possible that guide aspiration and behavior, thus do not encompass physics and calculus. Becoming an engineer—unlike becoming a doctor or a lawyer or an insurance salesman—has not been seen as a way up in the segregated Black community. These folkways developed in response to very real historical conditions, to the limited and at best ambivalent interactions between Blacks and technology in this country. Folkways, the "consciousness of the race," change at a slower pace than societal conditions do—and so a working strategy can turn into a crippling blindness and self-limitation.

Some Blacks—like my father, who worked for nearly fifty years in a factory that, ironically, moved at the end of his career from unionized high-wage Illinois to the low-wage Mississippi he left as a boy—have been able to operate within these narrow parameters, to accept slow and steady progress while positioning their children to jump into the mainstream. But Blacks are also Americans, and as such are subject not only to notions of a steady rise but also to the restless ambition that seems a peculiarly American disease. Not channeled to follow the largely technological possibilities for success in this society, Black folkways in my opinion have instead embraced the sort of magical thinking—entertainment like hip-hop and professional sports—that is encouraged by the media and corporations whose sole interest in Blacks is as consumers.

5.

YOU, TOO, CAN BE Michael Jordan, LeBron James, or Jay-Z—just buy the shoes, just have the right look. No need to study, no need to work, the powers that be are against you anyway. Too many young Blacks believe that they have a better chance of becoming Jordan, a combination of genes, will, talent, and family that happens every hundred years, than of becoming Steve Jobs, the builder of two billion-dollar corporations, the first one started with his best friend while tinkering in his garage. Both are nearly impossible to achieve, but there are thousands, perhaps millions, more tech founders than there are NBA players. They also don't dream of becoming programmers at Cisco Systems, a low-profile computer giant that hires thousands of new workers a year and scours the globe to find them. In the sort of statistic than both gives one pause and illustrates the breadth of the problem, only 1.5 percent of tenured computer science faculty in the United States are Black women. These sorts of disparities echo throughout engineering, physical science, and other scientific disciplines. As I lamented earlier, the very opportunities that would allow young Blacks to vault over decades of injury and neglect into the modern world go not simply unclaimed but unseen.

Mastery of technology is in my view second only to money as the true measure of accomplishment in this country, and it is very likely that by tolerating this underrepresentation in the technological realm, and by not questioning and examining the folkways that have encouraged it, Blacks are allowing themselves to be kept out of the mainstream once again. This time, however, they will be excluded from the greatest cash engine of the twenty-first century. Inner-city Blacks in particular are in danger, as "clean communities"—such as DuPage County, outside Chicago, and the beautiful suburbs that ring the decay of Hartford, glittering cybercities on the digital hill, the latest manifestation of the American Dream—shed the past and learn to exist without contemplating or encountering the tragedy of the inner city.

But all dreams end, and when we wake, we must face reality. Despite these trends and the dangers they imply, not all is lost. What might be accomplished by an education system that truly tried to educate *everyone* to excellence, not just the children of elites and of the suburbs? Why not a technological Marshall Plan for the nation's schools? Even in this time of fiscal constriction and resistance to public expenditure—at least, any expenditure that does not directly benefit those doing the spending—such a plan is feasible. What if *uber*technocrats like Bill Gates and Larry Ellison, the billionaire cofounder of Oracle, used their philanthropic billions to fund basic math and science education in elementary schools to equip the future, instead of giving away merchandise that essentially serves to expand their customer base? That would be a gift worthy of their accomplishments, and one of true historical weight in the life of the nation.

And Blacks must change as well. The ways that served their ancestors through captivity and coming to freedom have begun to lose their utility.

If Blacks are to survive as full participants in this society, we have to understand *and apply* what works *now*.

Because it's not getting any better. Think of it this way: there are those who might say that smartphones, and their concomitant tools, social media and the internet, are finally a technological innovation that is working in favor of Blacks. But I might, politely, ask to differ: Smartphones and social media have certainly helped Blacks organize and protest. They have made them and their allies ever more aware of injustices around the United States and have helped them cite and interpret patterns of injustice and discrimination. Whether it has meant something as grave as providing visual proof and spreading awareness of police misconduct in the George Floyd killing or helping identify the routine day-by-day discriminations and micro- and not-so-microaggressions of various "Karens," thus proving such incidents to be much more than folklore, smartphones and social media have been a useful tool in advancing the interests of African Americans.

But they have provided the same advantages to our enemies.

There would have been no Charlottesville without smartphones and social media, and I think it is safe to say that someone like the murderer of the nine praying innocents at Mother Emanuel Church in Charleston in 2015 probably would not have become radicalized without the internet. White supremacists and neo-Nazis around the nation have been able to organize and find common ground and funding, and even worse, they have been able to tap into global networks that allow them to find further support and depth of intent. So it is, at best, an open question as to whether smartphones, the internet, and social media have been a net gain for African Americans, or whether the tools will eventually be seen as joining the long line of other technological "innovation" that I am describing, something that harms us much more than it helps.

What is to be done? How do we as Americans, assuming we even want to, help prepare African Americans to cross this technological threshold that is dividing our society, and the next one, and the next that emerges in human civilization? It is and has always been the future, and Blacks, playing catch-up yet again, must reach for it if we are to have any hope of ensuring ourselves a place at the American table, which in actuality seems to be an unending game of four-dimensional musical chairs.

Reading, Writing,
and the Risks of Failure

1.

I WAS BORN ABOUT a hundred years after the emancipation of African American slaves and grew up in Illinois, a state that, for all of its obvious racial difficulties—to include the 1837 murder of Elijah Lovejoy, the 1919 Chicago race riots, the violence and social tragedy resulting from the assassination of Dr. Martin Luther King Jr., to name a few instances—had always been more tolerant of Blacks in ordinary daily life than were the South and other locales. While the 1960s and '70s of my childhood were tumultuous times of conflict and transformation in American society, I have considered myself fortunate to have grown up at exactly that moment in American (and African American) history and in a quadrant of the state of Illinois in which I was not subject to the daily harassment, terror, and threat to life that other Blacks my age were regularly experiencing in other parts of the country.

In my childhood in Northern Illinois, there was hope in the air, a sense that hundreds of years of aspiration and struggle were being rewarded. I, and many of the Blacks with whom I came of age, had a sense that we were living out the next chapter in a tragic but ultimately triumphal narrative. We believed that we were authoring racial redemption, fulfilling the dreams and almost unimaginable sacrifices of our ancestors.

That presentiment may have been premature. It is becoming increasingly clear to historians, social scientists, politicians, and everyday Americans that the legal status of freedom that was *felt* so near for African Americans is not necessarily coming to fruition. African American progress seems to have become a repeated pattern of "one step forward, two steps back," as nearly every advance has been met by a backlash more intense than the one before it—first Nixon, then Reagan, then Trump, not to mention the unrelenting assault on voting rights, racial equity, and social programs in health and education by right-wing politicians, "conservative think tanks," and media outlets. African Americans have come to understand that no Black advance—whether in Reconstruction, *Brown v. Board of Education*, voting rights, Title VI, or affirmative action—is ever secure or beyond question. Anything gained, even from Congress, *even from the Supreme Court*, can be rescinded. One could argue that de facto equality for African Americans—that is to say, equality lived out in socially and materially tangible ways and in health outcomes, graduation rates, net worth, and actuarial tables—has not only not yet been achieved, it may never be.

I will not engage in arguing about whether African Americans have achieved our freedom because I have come to believe that question is unanswerable: in fact, the older I get, the more I wonder what such a thing would look like. Instead, I want to examine something that may be more important: the expectation that most Americans shared throughout my childhood and adolescence that it was possible, through learning and hard work, to change your life—to radically elevate your station—if that was what you wanted. Education was the single most pragmatic way to realize your capabilities, to materially enhance your life. And that mindset is connected to one of the greatest of all American heroes, the one who issued the Emancipation Proclamation.

2.

IN RECENT YEARS, I have realized how much Abraham Lincoln meant to my childhood, and not just because I grew up in Illinois, where he often loomed like a second sun straddling the sky. Lincoln's biography was, along with Dr. King's insight and achievement, a lodestar in how young Anthony grew to see and interpret the cosmos of his world. He showed, as my father loved to say, how people could become more than they were.

It was through Lincoln, the greatest Illinoisan of them all, that I came to believe that education was *the* catalyst of advancement. Knowing that he—born in dire frontier poverty—had transcended those material limitations, educated himself, and, through unceasing labor and canny diligence, risen to become the president of the United States, commander of the Union Army, and abolisher of the institution of slavery in the United States was a gospel parable to me. I was a Black boy who was learning to think of himself as such from the books of Richard Wright, another Chicagoan with Mississippi roots. Figuring out, even as a child, how to move forward in an American society that was unknown and unmapped for my family was frightening but also thrilling. I cherished my position in my community as a pioneer, as someone who would forage and explore on their behalf, learn how America really worked, and then bring back that news. Lincoln proved to me that it could be done.

So I read biographies of Lincoln, watched movies and documentaries, pondered his speeches and debates as if studying scripture. I also studied the oratory of Dr. King, believing that he was a fated, unavoidable, triumphal echo of Lincoln's thinking and actions. I believed in the testament of these men's lives as if it were my one true religion. This faith guided me, at least for a while. I was able to earn degrees from the University of Notre Dame and Brown, something my parents had not imagined, although they had left Mississippi full of naive ambition. I achieved many of my own dreams, including being able to publish several books and to work in the film industry. I proved, at least to myself, that Honest Abe was right: if you worked as hard as you could, studied by the firelight, and didn't give up, anything was possible.

3.

WHAT I DIDN'T SEE, or perhaps saw and ignored, was that millions of Blacks were not making the gains that my family was. I also didn't see how little financial capital Black Americans had in aggregate inheritable wealth and how much that mattered in the brutal procedural calculus of mainstream American life. We Blacks had not inherited our share of the earth. Only time—and broadening experience—would cure me of my childhood myopia.

As I matured, I learned that the axiom of American life that "anything is possible" was codified shortly after Lincoln died by the author Horatio Alger, whose novel *Ragged Dick* was the first of many stories he published to instruct young boys from the margins of society in how to become respectable. These stories have an arc, deeply embedded in our culture and thinking, that is strictly patterned and always upward, designed to provide instruction and inspiration. We can see that trope of uplift repeated in stories as varied as the classic autobiographies of Booker T. Washington and Malcolm X and the wildly successful autobiographies of CEOs such as Lee Iacocca and Jack Welch, the memoirs of celebrities such as Mariah Carey and Michelle Obama, and the narrative accounts of military heroes such as Colin Powell or Norman Schwarzkopf. The story is always the same: an American starts out in life at a strict disadvantage, works incredibly hard, has just enough good luck, and emerges on the other side—successful, proverbially rich, and famous. Typically, deeply embedded in these stories is the notion that education is the key, the galvanizing factor in an otherwise miraculous ascent.

This story informed how I saw the world as I pushed myself forward, and it felt true. I read many of these auto-biographies, starting with those of Malcolm X and Iacocca, and inhaled memoirs on the bestseller list or by someone whose work or achievement I admired. This diet of biographies and memoirs helped with my self-conception. It seemed that almost anywhere I turned, someone—friend or stranger, teacher, coach, or nun—was willing to see me as I saw myself: an honest striver on the way to success in American society.

My parents had not had the benefit of a good education and all its corollary advantages. Born in Depression-era Mississippi under the most brutal conditions of Jim Crow segregation and poverty, my mother was able to graduate from high school, but my father was not able to finish even grammar school. Yet, to both of them, the Lincoln-Alger model was the only way of proceeding in life. As Michelle Obama wrote of her parents, who were equally dedicated and determined, my folks were "evangelists of education." Their belief in Horace Mann's definition of schooling as "the great equalizer of the conditions of men—the balance wheel of the social machinery" was unshakable. To them, educational betterment was an unalienable truth, one in which they had more certitude than they did that the sun would rise in the morning.

4.

MY LIFE MIGHT STAND as a model of the US education sys-tem, a Mississippian version of the American immigrant story. Yet this idea of education as the enabling condition of advance may be *the* American myth, the thing that undergirds our country's faith in meritocratic reward and upward social mobility. Education should be a society-wide net that catches all children, providing them with tools to take advantage of the economic opportunities that America seems to endlessly generate.

But we can see, in many if not most parts of our society, that those educational opportunities are not being generated any more—and not just in neighborhoods of poor Blacks and Latinos, but throughout the nation, including for large swaths of middle- and working-class whites. This failure to provide adequate public education to most Americans radiates throughout our society in devastating ways, including, for example, the violence of the MAGA Trumpism acolytes and other white nationalists, who often seem fueled by a sense of white grievance that springs from feeling trapped without viable futures as the sort of blue collar high-school-educated economic opportunity that once existed wanes evermore.

These aggrieved whites feel left behind by elitist "meritocrats," who are seemingly uninterested in Americans who are not from the coasts or top tier universities. This Vesuvius of grievance has been building for over forty years, since the Carter administration, and has gathered force and velocity since the advent of Trump, who has harnessed white discontent for political gain.

Public education has been a slow-motion failure, a quietly escalating emergency, and we have not begun to take the measure of its implosion until very recently. It has various root causes. In Chicago in 1991, for instance, a child at age thirteen had a 50 percent chance of not finishing high school. Such a dismal graduation rate could be attributed, among other things, to the ongoing tragedy of race in the United States, as much of the city's public school system was populated by uneducated Blacks from Arkansas, Mississippi, Louisiana, and Alabama, whose parents or grandparents migrated to Illinois to work in factories. That migration was followed by the deindustrialization and globalization of the 1970s, '80s, and '90s. (In a bleak historic irony, those families had migrated because of the industrialization of agriculture in the South.) Yet the disaster reaches further: even those Chicagoan children who managed to graduate in 1991 had terrible competency scores in reading and math.

Project that circumstance forward to the present. Think about those tens of thousands of children being unequipped to succeed or even function in an economy that has utterly and drastically changed during the intervening thirty years, moving from industrial manufacturing to symbol-derived information employment, which requires skilled literacy and numerate mastery, as well as the ability to interpret and manipulate concepts and ideas and to interact with others from various backgrounds with practiced soft skills. Then think about everything you've heard about the Fox News, GOP, and right-wing talking point and meme of "Chicago" as a place of endless gang wars and gun crime.

Might these circumstances be connected?

When the best working-person's jobs were shifting from companies like United States Steel and General Motors to companies like UPS and Federal Express, where an employee *had to be able to read and work with numbers*, the

Chicago public school system was generating thousands of functional illiterates.

The Chicago Public Schools (CPS) appear to be doing better as of late, having raised test scores closer to the national average. In 2019, 61 percent of CPS students met or exceeded the national average in reading, 57 percent in math. That's better, if not much to be truly proud of: six out of ten CPS students are meeting national standards. But such modest progress also suggests why many Americans have given up hope in education as the mechanism of self-betterment. In many regions of the country, especially those far from the coasts, even an associate's or bachelor's degree won't take you far since the industrial manufacturing base has declined so precipitously.

The variety of hopelessness that fuels MAGA Trumpism is also manifest in the opioid epidemic that has spread like wildfire in the last two decades. That crisis has worsened, according to National Institute of Health with the 2020 death toll of 68,630 greatly exceeded by the 2021 death toll of 80,411. Improvement in some places seems only to accelerate the opioid crisis in other regions. Shortly after Iowa learns to mitigate opioid deaths, the problem becomes epidemic in Idaho or Rhode Island or some other state. While the causes of opioid addiction are multifaceted, including patients beguiled into addiction while being treated for legitimate pain, many users pursue the high afforded by the narcotic for temporary escape or to alter their consciousness in the face of dim prospects.

This contributes to the American epidemic in "deaths of despair," as they have become known, as political, economic, and spiritual malaise lead to growing numbers of deaths from alcoholism, drug overdose, and suicide. The greatest numbers of opioid users (one may add methamphetamines to this discussion) map onto areas of deindustrializing and rural America, places with failing economies and subpar education systems. Those states that have had their tax bases hugely eroded by loss of industry—such as Ohio, Illinois, West Virginia, Wisconsin, Michigan, Iowa, and Pennsylvania—have high per capita deaths by overdose. Many of those same states are also struggling to pay for the educational attainment that they had provided in the not-so-distant past.

All this said, I am aware of the danger of oversimplification.

Many contingencies determine how educational opportunity will operate for any given American. Are your parents educated? Do you live in a locale that provides opportunity in general, for example, in suburban Boston or Northern Virginia as opposed to Jackson, Mississippi, or South Bend, Indiana? Do you have special needs, neurological or economic, and are those needs recognized and met by your family and your school system? For example, a child with neurodivergence is provided with exceedingly more educational support and practitioner availability in Massachusetts than in the neighboring New England state of New Hampshire. Are you a five-star athlete, which means that things will be overlooked or attended to because you can help a big university earn money through its athletic department? Are you from a skilled and informed upper-middle-class family that has the ability (and willingness) to pay for private resources that are not publicly provided where you live and the practical savvy to advocate for, if not demand, those resources? These contingencies can determine whether an American public education will work for you, if it will "balance," as Horace Mann had it, the social machinery.

But I am concerned about something deeper than our society's interest in providing educational opportunities that enable every American to progress economically, or to merely exist with pride and dignity. While we must think about education through economic and aspirational frames, we must also consider it through the civic frame of what makes our democratic society possible: the creation of American citizens.

Are our contemporary educational systems producing *citizens* who are equipped to meet the challenges put before them? I think, most obviously, of the humanistic and technological skill that enabled our country to meet the totalizing demands of World War II with equal parts gravitas and civitas that bound us together to combat totalitarianism and the Nazi campaign of genocide.

When I think of my own education, it meant more than just becoming a solid marketplace participant. It meant becoming a *citizen*, which meant knowing what made this country different and special, and what I had to do to live up to membership in this body politic. It meant thinking of the nation as something to which I *belonged*, something larger than me in which I was both obligated and honored (and fortunate) to participate.

Let me step back and ask an obvious question: what does it mean to be educated in the United States in 2024? We are, of course, familiar with general definitions and connotations of "education": to provide intellectual instruction or training in particular fields. But I have long been contemplating the notion that the purpose of education is to provide intellectual *as well as* moral and social instruction to individuals, and by extension to society as a whole.

Education implicates the great motto of the United States: *e pluribus unum*, "out of many, one." Fifty states with their various climates, histories, and cultures form one nation; countless institutions cohere into a unified, usually functioning whole that serves the nation's varied groups and alliances; hundreds of millions of individuals (most of the time) work together in the service of both themselves and of the whole. On the face of it, what the "many" in the United States have been able to accomplish as one over the last two hundred and fifty years, with all of our varied faults, is nearly miraculous.

Traditionally, Americans have seen education as the loom that enables the many to weave into one through a process we term "democracy." But has our system, celebrated for its ability to create economic success and achievement—including that of my own family—failed to respond to the burdensome legacy of the past and the demands of the twenty-first century world? If so, do we care enough to do something about it? Are we wise enough to recognize that if we don't, the entire American enterprise is threatened?

5.

ONE WAY OF THINKING about why education no longer works in the United States is relatively straightforward: Too many citizens encounter school and university systems that no longer provide what people need to succeed in a postindustrial information economy. The capabilities of those seeking employment, the skills needed in the jobs available, and what those jobs actually provide are often mismatched. (Think of the false promises of the gig economy, the now laughable notion that we could transition to an economy of folks living on—or supplementing lower- or lower-middle-class salaries or hourly wages with—their "side hustle," whether that was driving for Uber, walking dogs, doing chores, or renting out a guest room.)

This scramble for a sustainable income is no longer just a problem for African Americans and other people of color. It is a problem for large numbers of whites, too, and contributes to some of the tribal antagonism between these groups, fueling an economic conflict that often becomes racialized. This is one of the factors driving Trumpism, with all of its collateral damage for the nation. Rather than imagining a way forward and an America that is beneficial to all, Trumpists want to go *backward* to an imagined halcyon past in which many Americans were, in actuality, excluded and repressed, but large numbers of whites were economically ascendent—or at least think that they were. This nostalgia ignores various accidents of history that enabled the post–World War II era's once-in-a-millennium boom economy. It is difficult to overstate the benefit that the United States gained from being the last man standing after the Second World War—our economy and mainland infrastructure fully intact—with very little industrial competition until the early '70s.

Geography adds to the disparity. Coastal cities and blue states are generally doing well economically, rural states less so, unless, like Texas, they also contain economic powerhouse metroplex cities. Meanwhile, the jobs that the working class needs to earn a living wage are harder to come by wherever one lives. I think of my father and his friends, who were able to make middle- and even upper-middle-tier wages in manufacturing jobs, which provided them with pride, honor, economic power, and a sense of belonging— very few of which exist anymore. I think of the city I was born in, Aurora, Illinois, a manufacturing center for much of the late nineteen and twentieth centuries. Most of those companies are now gone. I think in particular of Allsteel, where my father worked for forty-two years, and Caterpillar, where I worked for two summers while I was in college. I also worked several lucrative summers at General Mills, another large operation in West Chicago that is now closed. Combined, those companies provided thousands of well-paying union jobs with great benefits. They are no longer there.

Tragically, these economic shortcomings spawn social tensions that are exacerbated by the failure of the education system to deliver not only the opportunities available in the thirty years after World War II but also a proper understanding of the history of the nation. This is further threatened by GOP attempts to limit what topics and facts of our political and social histories are taught. Not only has American education failed to prepare its citizens for the current economy, it has also failed in what should be the more readily accomplished task of helping Americans understand *change*, the most salient experience of American life.

Our nation is so dynamic it can be disorienting: nearly every ten years, we tear the country up and replace it with something completely new. Consider, for instance, the seismic change in our country's governance and policies from Obama in 2008 to Trump in 2016. And, prior to that, the radical shifts between Bush Sr. and Clinton, or Johnson and Nixon. This secondary failure—to teach our citizens how to think about and be equipped for change—helps account for the acceleration of violence we are witnessing in our political realm. Those existential threats that we, as human beings, cannot readily understand only exacerbate our worst tendencies—what appears, in various guises, as disillusioned apathy or thunderous rage. Think of what the great Anglo-Irish poet W. B. Yeats wrote in 1920 during the Irish War of Independence: "The ceremony of innocence is drowned; / The best lack all conviction, while the worst / Are full of passionate intensity." Poetry can, at times, double as prophylaxis or prophecy.

6.

WE CURRENTLY EXPECT AMERICAN public schools to provide children with whatever they have not been provided at home. The landscape of broken families, eviction crises, and a lack of nutritious food and sufficient health care in our troubled urban and rural areas is another complication we expect our schools to remedy.

Can we realistically ask public schools to serve as both social service agencies *and* purveyors of skills and knowledge?

From my perspective as a Black man, we have no more urgent national business than fixing our education system. If we don't solve this problem, we will end up with a much bigger one: a nation that is ungovernable, unable to perceive and apprehend itself, and unable to function just when we need to function with more efficacy and urgency than ever before. Chastened by the COVID pandemic, political polarization, and climate change, we cannot help but be alert to this national crisis, whatever position on the political spectrum we happen to occupy. The battle for facts—in education and public life—is the battle for a commonly acknowledged reality without which we cannot be a democratic nation. Thus, we must assess the grave risk to the country posed by the insurrection of January 6 alongside the relentless lies and misinformation of Trump and Steve "Flood-the-Zone-with-Shit" Bannon, as well as the absurdities of QAnon and other conspiracies driving civic disarray and disorientation.

We must have a common understanding about what is and is *not* American history. Ron DeSantis may or may not succeed with his fiat to teach that slaves "received personal benefit," but Black people, and many of their white, Latino, and Asian allies, will not concur, and if they have to they will set up schools to teach the truth. This has been done before, including in Mississippi and Alabama, during the Civil Rights Movement; those schools were known as Freedom Schools, and I would not be surprised to see them emerge again, by necessity. But that will result in two competing versions of our history, and we will march further down the cacophonous road of polarization.

What is the cost of not having a common history? Recently, the eminent scholar and journalist George F. Will admitted, in an interview with *Politico*, that he had not been familiar with the Tulsa Race Massacre of 1921—a two-day spree of terror, looting, murder, and arson in which mobs of white men rampaged through the Greenwood neighborhood of Tulsa, Oklahoma. Greenwood was a Black neighborhood so prosperous that it was referred to by Blacks throughout the nation as Black Wall Street. White mobs destroyed thirty-five square blocks of the city and murdered an estimated three hundred Blacks; the true number of Blacks massacred in that event might never be known: there are mass graves throughout the region, including several unearthed in the past few years.

I shudder to think what else someone as well educated as George Will does not know about such a recent and major piece of not only African Americans' or other minority groups' histories, but American history itself. He is a person I admire: a hard-nosed conservative intellectual whose values are not built from racial animus or contempt; he is a native of the Midwest who holds a doctorate in political science from Princeton University. On the other hand, I must say, without flippancy, that I am not surprised. Will, to his credit, admits that he should have known about the Tulsa Massacre. But his mea culpa is not shared by many of those whites protesting (and threatening) school boards, administrators, and libraries about what American society has long considered straightforward history lessons: facts they deliberately mislabel as "critical race theory." Tulsa is exactly the sort of story that DeSantis, on the one hand, and Ryan Walters, the chair of the Oklahoma State Board of Education, on the other, want to strike from the historical record. DeSantis and other right-wingers want to erase everything my family and ancestors suffered and act as though that history has had no effect on present circumstances.

Yet African Americans have known and discussed the Tulsa Race Massacre for generations: in addition to the three hundred Black Tulsans who were murdered, there were at least eight hundred left injured and twelve hundred homes destroyed. Insurance companies refused to pay the property loss claims on those homes, citing force majeure exclusions. The total loss for those policyholders who went to court exceeded $22 million (the equivalent of more than $375 million today), and they were but a small percentage of those who lost everything in that violent attack against one nucleus of Black economic power in the United States.

There was also the spiritual loss, which is incalculable. Physically, thirty-five blocks of the city were razed in one night and day of white-on-Black organized violent terror in a massacre that is a commonplace fact in African American history and, I will argue, an essential element of the African American psyche. Yet it is not part of most whites' historical knowledge. We must contemplate as a society the real-world implications of these conflicting memories.

Some white Americans who do not know about things like the Tulsa Massacre are startled to learn about the emotions, preoccupations, and even resentments that many Blacks carry to the present day based on this parallel yet suppressed history; consequently, they do not have the context to comprehend what is happening around them now, including Black disaffection.

These unaligned accounts—these conflicts in the historical narrative—have been subsumed into reductive politics, where to state the truth is somehow to endanger the feelings of white children. Blacks (and their allies) are bullied into silence, expected to submit to the theater of amnesia that enabled the Minneapolis Police Department to ignore decades of complaints by African Americans (as substantiated in reports by the State of Minnesota and the US Department of Justice) that culminated in the murder of George Floyd.

What if white and Black Minnesotans, grappling with the aftermath of that modern-day lynching, had been educated in the full story of our nation's history and were equipped, now, to listen to each other?

7.

THE LACK OF AN effective, comprehensive public education system—one that equips all of us with the basic skills of reading, writing, and math; with skills for being a citizen; with a knowledge of the actual history of our country—creates a crippling stasis in our society. We can't discuss or analyze problems that ought to be neutral, including our biggest looming crisis: the climate. In the same way that the COVID pandemic should not have been politicized, the climate crisis should be recognized by all Americans as a matter of science, subject to measurable observation and experiment. And it should be a condition of good citizenship to understand how science works and its role in our world.

I think of Jonathan Haidt, professor of social psychology at New York University, who speaks of "the constitution of knowledge," how we must agree *on what we know* so that we might know more. Too many people seem to think that they can embrace science when it benefits them—with iPhones, buildings and roads, Tylenol and antibiotics—and that they can dismiss it when it doesn't suit their aims or habits of consciousness. Concomitantly, we have lost the ability to engage with each other on difficult problems, which prevents us from creating solutions as we have during previous crises such as the polio epidemic, the Spanish flu, HIV, and World War II. We are unequipped to debate in an educated fashion, from a shared set of assumptions, that would enable us to grind through problems and devise workable solutions. Instead, we search for domination through emotion and violence, implied and actual, and, perhaps worst of all, through misinformation and lies, rather than forming consensus and implementing a shared plan.

I cannot blame the public education system for all of our failures as a society. Its failings are symptomatic of larger crises of race, class, history, science, and truth. There are many great unsaids in our society, and there are too many things that cannot be studied because they fall under the silencing penumbra of race. We don't discuss why, for example, Black children lag in various measured categories because people are afraid of seeming racist or don't want to interrogate their own privilege. Something similar adheres to class issues: What *is* the difference between going to a glamour high school (such as New Trier in Winnetka, Illinois) as opposed to going to a public school in a failing mill town with textbooks twenty years out-of-date? How does that effect your life chances? I suspect a lot of people don't really want to know.

If we do not face these questions, we will not be able to fix our education system, and if we can't fix education, we may doom ourselves to failure. The most cursory perusal of the Roman Empire reminds us that even the mightiest can fall.

8.

THIS BRINGS ME BACK to Lincoln, the little boy from the hinterlands who rose to be the most important person in our nation's history. Whenever I see the mug shot of a hardened criminal, Black, white, or other, I think about that person as a five-year-old, eager to learn and participate, just like the young Abe, who wanted to be *more* than the circumstances of his birth. I think about boys I knew growing up, not all of them Black or Latino, whom I knew did not have a chance. Many of them knew that too. They knew, even if only subconsciously, that society was willing to literally write them off, to declare them as without value. And when something is deemed worthless, you do not, to borrow another financial term, *invest* in it.

I think of a story I reported in Milwaukee in the '90s, and the young Black boys who seemed to know in elementary school that they did not have any prospects of success. While I don't think every criminal is created by society, I do think some of them are, and that others—Black, white, Latino, Asian, and Native American—are consigned to lives more limited than they might otherwise have been because of our failures as a society, especially in education. I think of those I knew as children who were doomed by a system that did not meet their needs—for sound instruction, specialized services, or the recognition that not everyone learns in the same way.

Looking around our nation today, I see Americans, young and old, who are not equipped, through no fault of their own, to participate and thrive in society. Their lives are the collateral damage of a public system that fails more often than it succeeds.

9.

I HAVE MENTIONED AMERICAN icons such as Abraham Lincoln, Horatio Alger, and Horace Mann; I will now quote another, Thomas Jefferson: "If a nation expects to be ignorant and free, in a state of civilization, it expects what never was and never will be."

I can think of no better argument or caution for the role of education, for why we must concern ourselves with rectifying the failures in our politics, in our news media and social media, and in our streets and roads, rural and urban. Once one internalizes Jefferson's truth, there's not much else to be said, although I will admit this: as crucial as I think education is to everything we are (*e pluribus unum*), have been, and will be as a nation, I don't know if it is the solution to everything.

I don't think, for example, that hardcore white supremacists or QAnon adherents will be *educated* out of their animus toward whomever or whatever they are angry about, and it will be difficult—if not impossible—to move that type of idealogue toward respectful facility with facts and accepted, peer-reviewed history. Grievances such as those displayed by MAGA, alt-right, white nationalist, and white supremacist adherents are akin to the unregulated emotions and lack of rationality that leads small children to have screaming tantrums. They have little to do with formal education and logical thought and more to do with the functions of the human amygdala, which is to say rage and inchoate longing, as well as the willingness of various bad actors to exploit that vulnerability of human neurology. Such manipulation supersedes the efficacy of this preschool ethos or that one, or of the skills unmastered at community colleges or in the Ivy League.

One basic way forward is to spend money equitably on education, first by allotting the same amount for the instruction of each child annually—Scarsdale, New York, at the time of this writing, spends $35,000 per child, while Chicago spends $16,000. But could such equalized spending even be contemplated, much less discussed? Is it something our society would truly value, a level playing field for all children? On the other hand, what is our future unless we do so? And I think we can, or could, afford a Marshall Plan for *our* nation. Consider how many trillions of dollars we've spent in Afghanistan (accepting that there was a serious need for severe police action there after September 11, 2001) and in Iraq over the last twenty-five years.

We have little to show for that investment. In fact, one could say we could have just piled up the trillions and set it on fire in the desert for what we have to show for it.

Imagine what could have been accomplished here in the United States had that money been spent domestically instead, educating our citizenry, helping the Silent Generation and the Baby Boomers interpret what was happening as the economy changed, and preparing Millennials and Generation Z intellectually, morally, and socially for the vocational challenges to come, for the crucible of the climate crisis, and for the challenges of good citizenship in modernity's flux. Add to all this the metaphorical meteor strike of the COVID pandemic, and we begin to see how the failures of our educational practices might become the seeds of our destruction.

We have to learn to talk to, listen to, and work with each other despite our moral and intellectual differences, large and small, including coming to understand that politics is a method for the mediation of differences, not the arena in which to employ gladiatorial combat in search of emotional satisfaction. Given the evidence and result of unceasing conflict put before us every day in Washington, in our state capitals, and in our local councils and boards, whatever we are doing at present to educate ourselves as citizens is not working. And those of us of privilege cannot continue to turn away from, or exploit, these failures to feather our financial nests and solidify systemic power.

We must reinvent education in order to rebuild our body politic.

Historical wisdom and experience—from the American Revolution and Emancipation to World War II and the Civil Rights and Women's Movements—affirm that we can achieve comity if we want to. Think of the renewed emphasis on science and technology during the space race of the 1950s and '60s and what was accomplished as a result. Think of all the subsidiary technological gains to our efficiency and pleasure, such as cellular phones, GPS, and the internet. We have previously altered our educational course when needed and have done the necessary things that allowed our society to regroup and move forward.

Will we this time?

I am startled to realize that uttering that question is a kind of confession. It is another lesson from the life of Abraham Lincoln, and perhaps education's greatest gift: the acquisition of *perspective*, a means of looking through the present moment with all of its threatening chaos to what has been accomplished over the country's first two centuries. My perspective—what I look through, as an African American and as a descendant of men and women who were enslaved and then entrapped in Jim Crow Mississippi—is what the Trumpists in our nation wish to deny and expunge. But the American past is inextricably entwined with the story of its African American citizens, and we cannot realistically imagine a peaceable future unless we have an accurate working record—a shared cultural memory—of that past.

Perspective allows us to imagine a sanguine future that might emerge if we recognize where we are and what needs to be done, just as Lincoln forged a path for himself from a shabby cabin in Illinois to the White House, and from there a path for the country from chattel slavery and civil war toward peace and a truer American freedom. Even a rationalist such as myself can acknowledge that perspective—or viewing things with a steady look backward as well as forward—has a way of offering, even in the face of grave national challenges, a way to strive on to finish the work.

Willie Horton and Me, Again

W HAT I THINK about as I reread "Willie Horton and Me," thirty-five years after it was first published, is the way it represents the end of my innocence as an American.

At that time, in the summer of 1989, I was beginning to realize that much of what I had been taught by my parents and aunts and uncles, by my teachers and mentors, was a half-truth, a myth intended to encourage me to continue the journey of my people, by which I mean African Americans from the Deep South of the United States, on their quest to greater participation in the fullness of American life and society. I don't think they intended to deceive, and I don't know that I blame them; they were in a tough spot. How do you tell a young person the truth when you know the truth to be so brutal?

As I stared at Horton's mug shot on television in the George H. W. Bush for President commercials and on the news, in newspapers and magazines, even in the recesses of my own imagination, I could unconsciously and intuitively feel that that photo, with its menace of "the other," was going to, in a trick of neuroscience, come to represent specifically me and every other young Black man I knew, more broadly Black people in general, and that the photo would come to be an avatar of so many young Black men and women who have since died unjustly at the hands of the police and race-addled private white citizens. That photo boiled everything down to its essence: we were, and are, a threat. We are *the* threat, perhaps only rivaled in the imagination of a certain kind of Trumpist-Tea Party-MAGA white person by immigrants from Mexico and Central and South America. Horton's aggrandizement in political advertising as an icon, as a specter of the lawless African American was blunt dehumanization, and it was most chilling to me because this image, this stereotype, was being put forward by men, including then Vice President George H. W. Bush and his staff, who purported to be stewards of the nation.

Think of it this way: when the heinous Charles Manson, or the despicable Richard Speck, the coward Dylann Roof, or Roy Den Hollander, the 2020 double murderer of the husband and child of a federal judge, or any other white criminal is portrayed in the media, they are not then projected as representative of all other white males and a putative dire existential threat to our communal well-being as a community and nation. It is not implied that they, in particular, in their mere existence, represent a threat that one half of the political structure (the Democrats) cannot be trusted to control and contain. It is not even implied that white males *need* to be controlled and contained, though, given the activities that some of them are accused of, such as the murder of Ahmaud Arbery, the plots to kidnap Governors Gretchen Whitmer and Ralph Northam, the murders in Charleston, the violence at Charlottesville, the insurrection of January 6, and on and on, one might argue that they need to be. No, the crimes that white men commit are presented as tragedy, oddity, quirks in human nature, sociological problems to solve and remediate. Willie Horton, on the other hand, was presented as a threat to the very fabric of our nation's existence; by implication, he was representative of all Black men, and, ergo, how Black men and women also represent, *embody*, that fatal threat.

And I do not think this is an exaggeration.

But I am getting ahead of myself. When I wrote "Willie Horton and Me," a year after the 1988 campaign, I was becoming aware of my true place in American society, and that no matter what I did, or how I acted, or whatever I accomplished, a significant percentage of Americans would link me to him. It would be years before I would learn various salient facts around how that benighted man, Willie Horton (even the name rings like a southern cliché as it conjures a demented outlaw "darky"), gained his place in our mythology and folklore. *But I was starting to feel it.*

When I wrote the essay, I didn't know that the advertisement was a deliberate and intentional maneuver by 1988 Republican presidential campaign strategists to "sow the wind," to borrow a metaphor from that scripture so beloved by white evangelicals, and gain political advantage by inciting the fears and paranoia of just enough white voters to tip the election in their favor. I had my suspicions, which I adumbrated in the original essay, but those suspicions would be confirmed by one of the architects of the strategy, Lee Atwater.

Shortly before his death in 1991, Atwater rather clinically explained to political scientist Alexander Lamis what he and his fellow strategists were thinking as they developed the ad: "You start out in 1954 by saying, 'N----r, n----r, n----r.' By 1968 you can't say 'n----r'—that hurts you. Backfires. So you say stuff like forced busing, states' rights and all that stuff. You're getting so abstract now [that] you're talking about cutting taxes, and all these things you're talking about are totally economic things and a byproduct of them is [that] Blacks get hurt worse than whites. And subconsciously maybe that is part of it. I'm not saying that. But I'm saying that if it is getting that abstract, and that coded, that we are doing away with the racial problem one way or the other. You follow me—because obviously sitting around saying, 'We want to cut this,' is much more abstract than even the busing thing, and a hell of a lot more abstract than 'N----r, n----r.'"

I think that stands as evidence; one of the two major American political parties has deliberately, for more than fifty years, fanned the fires and divisions of racial hatred and misunderstanding. *As their plan.*

Consider a statement made by Trump supporter Crystal Minton, who said to *New York Times* reporter Patricia Mazzei in reference to Donald Trump, "He's not hurting the people he's supposed to be hurting." She was complaining that the 2018–19 government shutdown, implemented by Trump, was harming her and the people of her small town, who were largely dependent on government jobs at the federal prison in their town of Marianna, Florida. In Minton's statement, we hear the revenant of Atwater's remark: "Blacks get hurt worse than whites."

But by 2019, the subtext had become the text. Atwater had played a very large role in this GOP battle plan, often referred to as the Southern Strategy, architected in 1968 by the Nixon campaign to use race as a wedge issue. But I didn't know that, not for sure, in 1989. In 1989 it was painful and bewildering. And looking at it from the vantage point of 2024, I didn't know that not only would it continue over the next thirty years, but it would get ever more sophisticated and savage, turned to cringing effect against Barack Obama, and finding (one must hope) its apotheosis in the mind-numbingly regular statements and taunts of Donald Trump. I have to say, as an intellectual proud of what I think of as my sophisticated irony, it would almost be funny, like a *Saturday Night Live* or Dave Chappelle skit mocking outdated ignorance, if I were not the parent of a child who has had her childhood blighted by all this.

I also didn't know as I wrote, and neither did many others, that the officer who apprehended Horton and brought him to justice, Yusuf A. Muhammad, was African American. Muhammad, a corporal in the Prince George's County Police at the time, shot and wounded Horton while bringing him in. That wasn't in the ad. It also wasn't in the ad that Corporal Muhammad was the recipient of two degrees from Johns Hopkins, that he would go on to be a police chief, or that he would finish his illustrious career with the Metropolitan Police of Washington, DC.

The everyday occurrence that the best and worst of our society, a valiant *and studious and learned* police officer and a vile criminal, were of the same race had been conveniently overlooked by the Republicans in their rush to stereotype Black males. And perhaps it points to what I have come to think of as the general incompetence on these matters of the Democratic Party and their strategists that they did not make an advertisement pointing this out. Instead, we were left with a masterpiece of cruel political magic stirring up fear and division that went virtually unanswered and that has been allowed to morph and metastasize over the succeeding decades.

Everything I have written up until this point is context: I think it is extremely important that we, all of us, remember just how big and deliberate all the circumstance involving and surrounding "Willie Horton" was. You can call me naive, or you can call me the son of parents who believed in American possibility, or who had no choice but to believe because they had nowhere to go but up. We were, as a family, from the fields of Mississippi, caught up in the Great Migration, so we embraced opportunity wherever we could find it and kept pushing, trying to make a place in America for ourselves and for our descendants. And we, basically, did.

But we also paid a price, as we had to become detached, even cynical, as we learned what too many of our fellow citizens thought of us, and as we continue to learn today. In our minds, we carry a skein of voices, the poignant pleas of African Americans for their lives and the brutal assertions of white supremacy:

I can't breathe.

There were fine people on both sides.

He's not hurting the right people.

In 1989, I was naive. I did not understand that there were substantial numbers of American whites who were basically unpersuadable on the issue of racial equality, who would view any progress or advancement by African Americans and other Americans of color as a setback for themselves, who would embrace stereotypes and unfair castigation. And by saying I *was* naive, I don't mean to imply that I have by now figured things out. I am regularly startled and often surprised by things that happen in the racial realm in our country, and I have come to realize over the intervening decades that what can only be described as white supremacy—the belief that America is, ultimately, of, by, and for the benefit of people with skin that is described in our vernacular as white—is inscribed in the metaphoric DNA of our nation.

In my belief, that mode of thinking is so deeply inscribed in the genetic material of our nation that it will not—cannot—ever be fully excised. It is something that we, those who do not believe in or support the doctrine of white supremacy—Black, white, Latinx, Asian, Indigenous—have to regularly, constantly, fight against.

Unfortunately, one of my ways of fighting has been to learn to avoid situations that can become humiliating, provocative, or stressful—situations where I cannot, will not, be seen as an individual. Rather than push against an

insurmountable wall, I have wagered that is it better to develop a detachment that preserves psyche, soul, and blood
pressure. This particular lesson was hammered home to
me by an incident that occurred years after "Willie Horton and Me" appeared. I had scheduled a lunch with my
close friend who was a celebrated psychiatrist and fellow at
Rockefeller University in New York City. We were scheduled to have lunch at Rockefeller that day, where we would
sit down with, among others, the renowned physicist Mur-
ray Gell-Mann.

So maybe I was feeling a little full of myself, thinking
that I was moving ahead in the world. Maybe I was forgetting the lessons I had learned, because I was in Lower
Manhattan as lunchtime approached and needed to get to
the Upper East Side location of New York Hospital, where
I was to meet my friend and walk to lunch. But, as I relate
in the original essay, I needed a cab.

Suffice it to say, I did not secure a cab ride, even though
I was expensively, in my mind exquisitely, attired in a suit,
with the same trim military style haircut. The rest can be in-
ferred by what I describe in 1989. What was different in the
incidents is that when I finally made it to our rendezvous,
running late for lunch, my psychiatrist pal stopped me and
asked why I was so angry. I said, "You know why I'm angry."

"*Why* are you so angry?" he asked, again, calmly and
firmly.

"You *know* why I'm so angry," I said, again.

"Anthony, are you a masochist?" the good doctor said
seriously, and with a hint of the levity that was a feature of
our friendship. I told him I didn't know what the hell he
was talking about. But he did. He said, "Listen. You know

what is going to happen if you try to get a cab. Yet you counted on getting a cab. Why didn't you take the bus? Ride the subway? Walk?" He looked at me carefully, with both concern and love. "Why are you risking your health by fighting something you can't change?"

In that instant I began to understand what African Americans call, among ourselves, the "Black Tax," which is not only what we have to do extra but also what we *cannot* do, what we must accept. And I can't get a cab, or do any number of other things because of what too many people think about Willie Horton, which is part of what they think about Black men, and Black women.

So I leave early. I take the subway. I walk. I make sure I don't "scare" anyone in the subway or supermarket parking lot after dark (or in daylight), even though what I am is a bookish middle-aged duffer mostly concerned with getting home so I can have some decaf and read novels.

I don't know or, perhaps more accurately, haven't decided, whether or not this sort of racial prudence constitutes a loss of liberty because it also counts in my book as a loss of liberty to endure suspicion, emotional assault, and deliberate humiliations. So why not avoid them if you can? And perhaps, in this current national context of renewed racial hostility, as reinforced by a recent president who smirkingly told the white supremacists to "stand by," this is not just weary prudence but active self-preservation.

I have realized that we African Americans often have to live inside the paranoid or delusional psychomachia of those whites who are preoccupied if not deranged by race. I think of the unarmed Black man in Minnesota, gunned down on May 1, 2020, by a white man after a minor car accident, just weeks before the murder of George Floyd. The gunman was twenty-four and claimed to be "in fear for his life," a statement vehemently disputed by witnesses and Good Samaritans at the scene.

The unarmed man who was murdered was named Douglas Cornelius Lewis. His death wasn't filmed, so it did not join the legion of martyrs that we as a nation know about and grieve. According to the *St. Paul Pioneer Press*, Mr. Lewis, a father of four and delivery driver for Amazon, had exited his vehicle after a fender-bender and was approaching the other vehicle when he was shot, by the other driver, from ten feet away.

It's astonishing to discover, as I did decades ago, and then be reminded—yet again—that one's mere conduct of daily life can provoke outrage, fear, contempt, and even murderous violence. And that has to do, still, I think, with Willie Horton as the apotheosis of a vision of Black persons born out of the crime of slavery, propagated through the centuries, and deployed until this day. And I don't have any solution. And I don't have any plan, other than to train my child for what she will face, to teach her what we African Americans have always taught our children about love, strength, and resilience, because it has become clear to me that this circumstance, four hundred years in the making, is not going to go away.

Acknowledgments

This book came as a surprise to me: for that, I have to thank my editor and friend, Joshua Bodwell, for his unflagging enthusiasm and granular meticulousness. I also thank Heather Treseler for her contributions, personal and professional, unceasing. Both of them saw possibilities for this book before I did, and then did heavy lifting to help it come into being. For that, I say thank you, much more than you know, and "without whom."

I also have to thank the editors of the original versions of many of these pieces, including Eric Copage, Patricia Towers, Kerry Temple and the *Notre Dame Magazine* team, Matthew O'Donnell, Marc Smirnoff, Farrell Evans, Jack Beatty, and for conversations, Nitsuh Abebe. I would like to thank our copy editor, Beth Blachman. And thank you to Gary Fisketjon.

Deborah Murphy is another without whose belief, assistance, and efforts this book wouldn't exist.

For support and belief over almost three decades, I would like to thank the members of the English Department, administration, staff, students, and community at Bowdoin College; especial thanks to Elizabeth Muther, Craig McEwen, Jennifer Scanlon, Franklin Burroughs, Mark Foster, Ann Kibbie, and Roy Partridge.

I thank friends Jeffrey Peterson, Moreen Halmo, Wayne and Marcia Beach, Jenny Manier, Richard and Kristina Ford, Matthew Greenfield, Charles and Patricia Russo, Gary Lawless and Beth Leonard, Chad and Susan Olcott, Tamsyn Leigh Bodwell, John Wright, and especially Valerie Upham, whose steadfast kindness and trust helped make this book possible.

Thank you and love to the Murphy Family, including Quentin and Susan, Peter and Babette, Elizabeth and Michael Fitelson, and young ones Helen, Margaret, Amanda, Tom, Quentin II, and Megan.

And to the Stern Family: Paul, Susan, Joshua, and Elizabeth.

None of this would have happened without the friendship, push, support, cheerleading, challenge, and belief of the late Michael S. Harper.

I would also like to speak to the memory of my friend John "Jack" Gleason, a model of American courage and probity throughout a life that ended too soon. Chris Leh, thank you for thirty-five years of dailiness, and George Makari, Egyptology, dude.

And thank you and love everlasting to my brother and sister, Timothy and Claudette; we have been rocking, literally, for sixty years, and I cannot imagine my life otherwise. May we continue to honor the memory and unfathomable love and sacrifice of Claude and Dorothy.

A NOTE ABOUT THE AUTHOR

Anthony Walton is the author of *Mississippi: An American Journey*, and editor, with Michael S. Harper, of *The Vintage Book of African American Poetry*. He is also coauthor, with Kareem Abdul-Jabbar, of the bestselling *Brothers in Arms: The Epic Story of the 761st Tank Battalion*, among other books. His writing has appeared in *The New Yorker*, *New York Times*, *Harper's*, *Atlantic Monthly*, *Black Scholar*, *Oxford American*, *Times Literary Supplement*, *Poetry Ireland Review*, *Notre Dame Magazine*, and *The Library of America: African American Poetry*, among many others. He has appeared on NPR, CNN, CSPAN, and the BBC. The recipient of a Whiting Award, he teaches at Bowdoin College.

A NOTE ON THE TYPE

The End of Respectability has been set in Goudy Old Style. Designed by Frederic W. Goudy for the American Type Founders in 1915, the old-style serif typeface takes inspiration from printing during the Italian Renaissance. The diamond shape of the dots of the i, j, and punctuation points give the sturdy typeface an eccentric touch. Goudy was perhaps the best-known and most prolific type designer of his era: by the time he passed away in 1947, he had designed 122 typefaces.

Book Design & Composition by Tamsyn Leigh Bodwell